Walking with God

Devotional

By

Tiffany Root &
Kirk VandeGuchte

Walking with God
1 Year Devotional

Copyright © 2022 by Tiffany Root and Kirk VandeGuchte

All rights reserved.

Edited, formatted, and published by
Destiny House Publishing, LLC.
P.O. Box 19774
Detroit, MI 48219
inquiry@destinyhousepublishing.com
www.destinyhousepublishing.com
404.993.0830

Cover by Kingdom Graphic Designs

This work may not be used in any form, or reproduced by any means, in whole or in part, without written permission from the publisher or author. Unless otherwise stated, all scripture is from the New King James Version (NKJV)

Printed in the United States

ISBN: 978-1-936867-79-0

WALKING WITH GOD

By Tiffany Root & Kirk VandeGuchte

Introduction

The Lord desires His people to hear His voice! As you read this devotional, listen for the voice of the Holy Spirit. If you've never heard the voice of the Lord, we believe this devotional will help you to hear the One who calls you. If you already hear Him, we believe that this devotional will enhance and improve both your hearing and relationship with Him.

Some devotionals are very short. Others are longer. Regardless, we hope you listen for the Lord's voice and journal what you hear. We have created this devotional with room to journal for that purpose. The journal can be found at the end of the devotionals before the index. You may want to write the devotional date and title next to your notes so you can refer back to it if needed.

We've also broken the devotionals up into categories, that we hope will help you if you ever need to look back at them.

May the spirit of wisdom and revelation be upon you as you read these devotionals. God bless you.

Tiffany & Kirk

Categories

1. Hearing God 1
2. Knowing God 31
3. Baptism 65
4. Holy Spirit 82
5. Gifts of the Spirit 107
6. In Christ 129
7. Wisdom & Revelation 167
8. Law of the Spirit 197
9. Prayer 224
10. Love & Faith 243
11. Discipleship 284
12. Healing & Deliverance 273
13. The Church 359
14. Children 399

HEARING GOD

JANUARY 1

The Lord says, "I have wanted a relationship with each of you since before Time began."

Read: Deuteronomy 28:1-2, 15   Matthew 4:4
          Deuteronomy 8:3   Ephesians 1:4

God calls Himself "Father" for a reason. He desires a family, and for you to be a part of it. He longs for you to know Him and love Him as He knows and loves you.

Jesus ties together the Old Covenant and the New Covenant in Matthew 4:4 and Deuteronomy 8:3. We have been chosen to be in Him <u>before</u> the foundation of the world, all because of love. He loves us and desires a relationship with us.

How do we get to know God, unless we listen to Him? In Jesus, we become children of God, and through His Spirit we commune with our Father, hearing Him and speaking to Him.

Deuteronomy 28:2 talks about blessings literally coming upon you, catching up to you and running you over! This is what God desires for you.

Command Satan to be removed from your presence, and ask the Lord if there's anything He desires to say to you regarding these things.

JANUARY 2

God has known you for all time, and yet He desires to speak with you!

Read (NKJV): Psalm 139:16   Jeremiah 1:5   Isaiah 46:10
Ephesians 2:10

It's pretty difficult to get to know someone and have a relationship with them if you don't talk with them. Even though God has known you before time began, He still wants to talk with you. He doesn't ever tire of talking with you, even though He knows you pretty well already! He wants to know you more intimately and have you know Him. He has great plans for you and loves you so much. His desire for you is even greater than your desire for Him.

Command Satan to be removed from your presence and ask the Lord if there's anything He desires to say to you regarding these things.

JANUARY 3

How do you start a listening prayer?

Read: Matthew 28:18   Luke 10:19

Jesus took authority from the enemy and gave it to those who follow Him. Therefore, you have authority in Christ, and that's why we start our listening time by commanding the enemy to go away and not speak to us.

Once the atmosphere is clear from the enemy's voice, you can then start listening for God's voice. As you get more and more familiar with the voice of Jesus, you will recognize when it's the enemy. He sometimes may say the same things God will say, but there will be an edge to his voice.

So, get rid of him when you listen!

Command Satan to be removed from your presence and ask the Lord if there's anything He desires to say to you regarding these things.

JANUARY 4

Will you give up your own thoughts to hear My voice?

Read: Ephesians 4:22-24   Luke 9:23   Romans 6:6-7

What we think or what we want can sometimes get in the way of hearing what God is saying regarding a matter. We need help giving up our thoughts. But if we come to the Lord and tell Him we give up what we think and only desire Him, we've then laid a good base for hearing Him. He knows our hearts and desires for us to hear Him, even more than we desire it. We can then command the enemy to be silent and listen for His voice in peace.

After reading the above scriptures, read 1 Corinthians 2, and then ponder the deep things of God, believing you have the mind of Christ.

JANUARY 5

The still small voice.

Read: 1 Kings 19:11-12   1 Samuel 3:2-15

The still small voice is the voice of God we most often hear. Why? (hint: faith)

Learn to recognize the still small voice. One way is to take a sheet of paper and write on one side: "My thoughts" and on the other side: "His thoughts." Under each column, write down what comes to mind. You will soon discern the still small voice which you will "hear" in your mind.

Command the enemy to be silent as you do this.

A great short book of testimonies regarding hearing God is Mary Geegh's book entitled, *God Guides*.

JANUARY 6

Come and council with Me you who desire justice; present your case.

Read: Genesis 18:16-33   Exodus 32:1-14

Righteousness and justice are the foundation of God's throne. He is always right, and He is always just. He has put the desire for what is right and just within us as well. Those who are His children, He trains to make righteous and just decisions, to notice when there is a lack of justice, and to see justice done.

This is why the Great I Am would take counsel with men. He's training us because as the Scriptures say, we will even judge angels. When we intercede for the cause of justice, the Lord will hear us. He leads us in what to pray by His Spirit. He wants justice and will listen to our cries regarding it. From the Scriptures we read today, you could even say God would make deals with men as He trains us in the way of justice.

Command Satan to be removed from your presence and ask the Lord if there's anything He desires to say to you regarding these things.

January 7

My words come with the power to perform themselves.

Read: Numbers 23:19   Hebrews 6:18

The word of the Lord does not fail and will accomplish the purpose for which He sent it. His words are powerful because they are Spirit and Life. The Holy Spirit is the power of God. If His words are Spirit, then they are power.

Additionally, God cannot lie. A lie has no power unless you believe it. A lie loses any power it had through deception once it is exposed to the light. The Lord's words are light. The very fact that God cannot lie means His words are always light and always Spirit. They come with the power to perform themselves.

God doesn't need to try to get His words to come to pass. He speaks and it's done. Whether we see it happen right away or not, His word is accomplished when He speaks. Amen.

Command Satan to be removed from your presence and ask the Lord if there's anything He desires to say to you regarding today's devotional.

JANUARY 8

Speak with Me and I will show you real peace.

Read: Isaiah 26:3   John 16:33

The Lord says faith comes by hearing. So, when we hear Him, we receive faith. Have you ever noticed that when your faith increases, so does your peace?

If we know that God's words cannot fail, then we have every reason to have peace when He speaks to us; and no reason to not have peace once we've heard His voice. Keep your attention on the Lord, and He will keep you in perfect peace. As your attention is focused on Him, you will be listening for His voice. You will hear Him, and you will have peace.

Command Satan to be removed from your presence and ask the Lord if there's anything He desires to say to you regarding these things.

JANUARY 9

Whatever the Holy Spirit hears from Jesus, He speaks to you.

Read: John 16:13-14

If the Holy Spirit is speaking what Jesus says, and Jesus is the Way, the Truth, and the Life, what would that mean for you? Would you ever hear something not true from the Holy Spirit? Could He possibly lead you astray? Would He ever lead you down the wrong path?

Remember that Jesus is the Way, the Truth, and the Life. So, if the Holy Spirit is bringing to you what He hears from Jesus, then whatever He hears will be according to the Way, the Truth, and the Life. He can't do otherwise. You can hear the voice of Jesus through the Spirit of Jesus, the Holy Spirit.

Command the enemy to be silent and ask the Holy Spirit to bring you what Jesus wants you to hear today.

JANUARY 10

My sheep hear My voice.

Read: John 10:27

This is such a comforting statement. *"My sheep hear My voice."* We can rest assured that we hear the Lord's voice. Some people say, "Well, I can hear my own thoughts and I can hear the devil's thoughts, but I can't hear God." No way! If you're able to hear any other voice, you certainly can hear the voice of Jesus.

And you don't need physical ears to do it either! God speaks to our hearts. Even unbelievers have heard God. Then, as His own, you certainly hear Him. He doesn't even say that you **can** hear Him, but that you **do** hear Him. It's a certainty.

Get rid of doubt and unbelief; and believe you hear God! Jesus said the Holy Spirit would bring to us the things He says. So, agree with God that you hear and listen for Him to speak today!

JANUARY 11

My sheep will not follow another.

Read: John 10:1-5

Remember the Scripture passage that says that a good tree bears good fruit? And a bad tree bears bad fruit? A good tree cannot bear bad fruit and a bad tree cannot bear good fruit. (Matthew 7:17-18) Do you know why this is the case? It's because when we're born again, we are given a new heart, and it's a good.

So, when Jesus says that His sheep won't follow another, He means it. Our hearts have been made good. You can rest in Him and that the Holy Spirit leads you into all truth. He doesn't lead us astray. We will recognize the voice of our Shepherd and not follow another voice.

Even if we're fooled momentarily, a good tree bears good fruit; so a good tree, or a good sheep, will turn away from the other voice as soon as it recognizes it and follow the voice of its shepherd.

If you look at yourself, you're not going to come away with faith that you won't be fooled into following another voice. But if you look at Jesus, you will come away confident that He will not lead you astray. He will speak to you and keep you on the narrow path. Believe Him when He says, *"My sheep will not follow another."*

JANUARY 12

I speak to you by My Spirit.

Read: John 14:26   John 15:26   John 16:13-15

So then, the Holy Spirit speaks only what He hears. He takes what is from Christ, and Jesus said all things that are the Father's are His, so He takes all things and declares them to us!

There is so much more to God than what is written in the Bible. He wants us to know the deep things according to 1 Corinthians 2. God is so much more than has ever been written in all the books, including the Scriptures.

We must cultivate that relationship with the Holy Spirit because Jesus speaks to us, through His Spirit. While it is true, we can tell the difference when it is Father speaking, the Son speaking, or the Spirit speaking. We still hear it all through the Spirit of God.

Praise Jesus for His Holy Spirit!

JANUARY 13

I Am the Word; I will not withhold My voice from you.

Read: John 1:1-2   Revelation 19:11-13   John 10:27

Jesus Himself is the Word of God. He is also the Good Shepherd. He will not punish you by withholding His voice. How could He do that? He took your punishment on Himself, and He says that His sheep hear His voice. He says He's the Word of God. He is not withholding His voice from you.

The very essence of being the Word of God means that He speaks. He even said in the Gospel of John that His words would judge us. (John 12:48) Well, in order for His words to judge us, we have to hear them. Even the unbelievers will be judged by His words, so even they can hear Him. And if the unrighteous can hear Him, then you, who are actually in Christ, can definitely hear Him!

So, rejoice today and praise Him that He will **not** withhold His voice from you!

JANUARY 14

I AM the Word; I will NOT be silent.

Read: Psalm 29

If He has a voice, we can hear Him. He is not silent, and therefore, you can always hear Him. There are no excuses. It is true the enemy lies to us and tries to get us to think we can't hear God. It's true that we get distracted from listening. It's true that we may hear differently from someone else, or He may tell us different things from our neighbor. based on our calling or gifting. However, none of those things mean that you can't hear Him. The Word speaks and is not silent. You, therefore, can always hear Him!

Declaration: I praise You, Jesus, that I *always* hear you! I am not going to give into the lies of the enemy that tell me I can't hear You for some reason or that You won't talk to me. Those are lies and I expose them as such! I declare that I hear You. I always hear You because You are the Word and You will NOT be silent! Amen.

JANUARY 15

I Am the word; I Am not a book.

Read: John 5:39-40

As we read, the Scriptures bear witness of Jesus, but Jesus is the Word. In fact, you won't find one instance of the Scriptures being referred to as the "Word" in the Bible.

First Peter 1:23-25 (NIV) reads,

> *For you have been born again, not of perishable seed, but of imperishable, through the living and enduring word of God. For, "All men are like grass, and all their glory is like the flowers of the field; the grass withers and the flowers fall, but the word of the Lord stands forever." And this is the word that was preached to you.*

Jesus is the imperishable seed. He is the word preached to us. We weren't born again from Scripture, but from the Word, Jesus. He is the Way, the Truth, the Life. We cannot come to Father apart from being born again from the Word, who is Jesus.

The Lord wants us to think of the purpose of the Scriptures. They serve to testify of Jesus. But they are not Jesus, nor can they replace Him. We can memorize the whole of Scripture and still not know God. For Jesus said that eternal life is to know God and Jesus Christ whom He has sent. We cannot have a relationship with a book.

Prayer: Father, thank You for the Scriptures that testify of Jesus. But thank You even more for Your Son, Jesus, who is the Word of God! Amen.

JANUARY 16

Heaven and earth will pass away, but My words will by no means pass away. Matthew 24:35

Read: 1 Peter 1:24-25   John 1:1 & 14

How is that God's words will never pass away? How can everything else burn up, but His words never pass away? Is He talking about the Bible? Couldn't that burn up? So, it must be more than that.

Remember that Jesus is the Life. And Jesus is the Word of God. So, everything that flows from Him is Life, and Life Eternal. Peter said to Jesus one time, "Where would we go? You have the words of eternal life." (John 6)

This is true. All we see around us will one day be gone. Nothing will last that we see. But the word of the Lord will last forever. His words are eternal because He is the very Word of God Himself, and He lives forever.

Therefore, what should hold our attention the most? Those things we see around us that will all pass away? Or, maybe those circumstances that bring pain and suffering? Or, should we pay more attention to the Word of Life and what's flowing out of Him?

We know the right answer. We simply have to choose Him. He doesn't want our attention taken by those things that pass away. He wants us to listen to His voice, His words, and believe Him. He is the Word of God so what He says is what remains. Amen.

Jesus is the Rock.

Read: 1 Peter 2:6-8   Matthew 7:24-27

Yesterday, we learned that Jesus' words will never pass away for He is the eternal Word of God. What do you see in common in these two passages we read?

Peter says those who stumbled over the Rock were disobedient to the word they had heard. And Jesus said whoever hears His sayings and doesn't do them is like those who built their house on the sand, not the rock.

We sing songs about how Jesus is our Rock, but do we really believe He is? Do we really listen to what He says and actually obey Him? If He is our truly our Rock, we will both listen and obey.

Talk to the Holy Spirit about the Rock today.

JANUARY 18

How did Jesus follow My Spirit?

Read: Matthew 4:4

Jesus said that we live on every word that proceeds from the mouth of God. That word "proceeds" means "currently proceeding." In other words, we live on every fresh word God speaks.

This then is how we follow the Holy Spirit. The Holy Spirit has been sent from God to lead us and guide us. He is the Comforter and Counselor. Jesus followed Him and sent Him to us that we may be filled with His same Spirit and follow Him too.

Jesus heard and obeyed. Therefore, this is what we do. We hear and obey. There's no other way to follow God than by hearing. And, hearing can be seeing as well. When we hear God, it may be a voice in our hearts, it may be a picture in our minds, it may be through a Scripture we read, or what someone else says to us. There are many ways to hear, but we follow by hearing.

JANUARY 19

How did Jesus teach, heal, and deliver?

Read: John 5:19   John 12:49-50

We've mentioned before that Jesus healed and delivered many different ways. How did He know what to do each time? Why didn't He just do the same thing over and over?

If we live on every word that God says, every freshly spoken word, then we're not doing things by the old word, but by the new word. Jesus only did what He saw Father doing, and He only spoke what He heard Father saying. He listened for the current word proceeding from Father's mouth.

This then is how we are to operate. We know that the Holy Spirit takes of what is Jesus's and declares it to us and Jesus said all things that the Father has are His. So, we listen for the voice of the Holy Spirit, and we say that. We look in the Spirit for what God is doing, and we do that. This is what Jesus did and this is what we do. It's how we operate as disciples of Christ.

Jesus taught by hearing and seeing, He healed by hearing and seeing, and He delivered by hearing and seeing. Can we manage any other way?

Who does the talking when you pray?

Read: Luke 6:12   John 12:49-50   John 16:13-15

How would Jesus know what to speak, unless He was hearing from Father through the Spirit of God? He spent time in prayer with God, but from what we read, it wasn't that He spent all night talking *to* God, but as we've talked about before, He talked *with* God. There's a difference.

Father wants us to make sure we do not come to Him and do all the talking. Jesus is the Word of God, so He speaks all the time. He wants us to hear Him. And His promise is that we **will** hear Him because the Holy Spirit brings to us whatever Jesus is saying. This is an awesome promise!

Therefore, when we pray, we need to spend more time listening than talking. Of course, Father wants to hear us, but there's so much for Him to tell us, we need to make sure we are listening for Him.

And when you have a question, wait for the answer from the Lord. Don't just ask things and then move on. Expect Him to respond. He wants to talk with you. He loves you so much!

JANUARY 21

Give your mind over to Me! Die!

Read: Romans 12:2   Ephesians 4:23   1 Corinthians 2:1

Jesus came to redeem body, soul, and spirit. However, even though we're born again, we need to practice taking our thoughts captive. The old dead man tries to resurrect and bring us the old thoughts and patterns we used to give in to. The enemy also tries to give us ideas that are contrary to the will of God. However, when we submit to the Holy Spirit, we die to those evil meditations and allow Him to bring us into the thoughts of God.

The way to give your mind to God is to take hold of the thoughts running through your mind and bring them to the Lord. For each one, listen to what He has to say regarding it. Then believe what He says. It may be your thoughts are good, for we have been given the mind of Christ. It may be that your thoughts need correction. If so, make the correction. The more you do this, the more the habit will be ingrained in you, and you will start to recognize by the Spirit of the Lord what comes from the throne of God and what does not.

When the Lord tells us to give our minds over to Him and die, this is how we do it. We die to our own thoughts, our own feelings, our self-centeredness as we give our thoughts to Him. Our mind belongs to Him, just like every other part of us. We can only live if we first die. So, if you want to live in the Spirit, you need to get ahold of your thoughts and you do that by submitting what you hear to the Holy Spirit.

Prayer: Holy Spirit, we give our thoughts over to You today. Correct us when our thoughts are not Your thoughts and bring us the thoughts of God. We confess we've been given the mind of Christ and we choose to live in those thoughts! Amen!

January 22

Does your mind wander?

Read: 2 Corinthians 10:3-5

Yesterday, we talked about giving our minds over to the Holy Spirit by taking our thoughts captive. This is the same thing we need to do when our minds wander.

Have you ever gone to listen to the Lord and your mind just wandered around? The Lord is saying to grab hold of every thought and individually submit them to the Lord. Tell that thought: "Not right now." Then go to the next thought. Do this until the thoughts are clear and you can hear the Lord.

Alternatively, you can ask the Holy Spirit about each thought as it comes through your mind. It may also help to take a piece of paper or a journal and draw a line down the middle of the page. On one side write, "God's thoughts." On the opposite side of the line, write, "My thoughts." This will help clear your mind so you can hear and will help you in recognizing His voice.

The Holy Spirit will help us take every thought captive and make it obedient to Christ. Ask Him to help you. He is called the Helper and the Counselor for a reason.

Prayer: Holy Spirit, help me today to take my thoughts captive, even the wandering thoughts. I submit my mind and my thoughts to you and receive the thoughts that come from you. Amen.

JANUARY 23

Learn to listen to My voice when you're under pressure.

Read: Luke 9:10-17   Luke 9:37-42

What we just read are two instances of Jesus hearing Our Father's voice under pressure. In the first instance, He could have gone along with what the twelve said to Him and sent the crowds away. There was pressure to do so. The people were in a deserted place and had been all day without food. However, Jesus didn't give into pressure, but listened and saw what Father was doing and did that.

In the second case, the pressure was to give into fear and unbelief. The disciples by this time had already cast out demons and healed sick people, but this boy they weren't able to help. Jesus had to give those thoughts of fear and doubt over to the Holy Spirit and listen to the Spirit's voice. What was God doing in this situation? Jesus did what He heard and saw Father doing. As a result, the boy was delivered and healed.

In both cases and in many more in Scripture, Jesus was under pressure, and He still heard, without getting anxious. Remember that He showed us how to live as a man (woman or child) filled with the Holy Spirit. He showed us how to follow the Spirit of God. He never gave in to pressure, but always stopped and looked and listened. We have the same Spirit in us that He had if we've been baptized into

Christ. So, don't give in to pressure, but allow yourself to listen to the Lord's voice even when the pressure is trying to come on you.

Prayer: Jesus, give us grace to recognize pressure when it comes and not give in.

JANUARY 24

Settling disagreements requires hearing God, but isn't that mainly for prophets? How do regular people follow what the Lord is saying?

Read: John 10:2-5   Hebrews 1:1-2

In the past, the way that God spoke was through His prophets. Now, however, it is notonly the prophets who hear God. Now, Jesus has come and has poured out His Spirit on all who are willing to carry Him. Now, we all can hear God without always having to go through someone else.

That doesn't mean prophets are done away with, however. While it is true that prophets hear for the church, He doesn't give everything to one person. God purposely causes each of us to need the others in the body of Christ. Therefore, God still uses His prophets to bring messages to His people. So, there are times when you will need to hear through someone else, especially through a prophet.

With that being said, it is also true that everyone can hear God and those in Christ do hear Him and follow Him, because Jesus said, **"My sheep hear My voice, and I know them, and they follow Me."** (John 10:27)

There are many ways to hear God, some of which are: a thought in your heart or mind, a picture or vision in your "imagination," a Scripture that is highlighted as you read, through a message you hear, or a friend who says something to you that the Holy Spirit "highlights," etc. God is so creative that if we tried to create an exhaustive list of ways to hear God, He would come up with something we never thought of before!

The point is that you can hear Him, and if you are in Christ, you *do* hear Him. Do not doubt; but believe. And believe the Holy Spirit is leading you into all truth, even into reconciling differences with your brothers and sisters in Christ.

When should children begin to hear God?

Read: 1 Samuel 3   Luke 1:13-17, 39-44

We just read two instances of children hearing God. In the first instance, Samuel was a young boy. The first time he heard God, he didn't even know it was the Lord. God hadn't spoken to him, yet. And it's interesting to note that the message he received was a very difficult one. He was afraid to speak the message to Eli. Eli threatened him with a curse if he didn't talk. Well, doesn't God know that's scary for a child? Samuel's first experience hearing God didn't give him the warm and fuzzies.

But God knows what He's doing. He knows what we can handle more than we do. He knows what our children can handle. He's not interested in coddling them, but in making them strong. He's very loving in all of it, but we can't be afraid to let our children hear God because of what He might say to them.

In the second instance we read, John received the Holy Spirit in his mother's womb! That's astonishing. And not only that, he was hearing God in his mother's womb. The Scriptures testify that he leapt for joy inside his mother's womb when Jesus came into the room and Mary greeted her cousin. This is a form of hearing God – when we are able to recognize the voice of the Lord through someone else.

There is no age required in hearing the voice of the Lord. At any age children can hear God, and they often hear Him very well because they do not have filters in place, yet, that would hinder that hearing. So, encourage your children to listen and to dream with God. And if you are a child, know that God has called you, and He wants to speak with you. Listen to Him, invite Him to play with you, and to dream with you – even in your daydreams.

Prayer: Father, praise You that You speak to all of us, no matter what age we are! Bless the children listening with greater faith and greater sensitivity to Your presence and Your voice. Fill them with such faith that they will never be talked out of hearing you, in Jesus' name, Amen.

KNOWING GOD

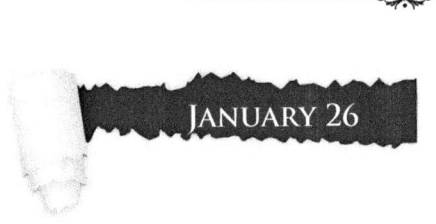

JANUARY 26

*I want people to know Me, not just about Me.
I want people to know Me.*

Can you sense the sadness of the LORD in today's statement? There are so many people who make it their mission to know everything about God, but they never actually know Him. In fact, they may even mock those who hear God, believing everything we could know is written in a book.

Jesus prays in John 17:3 (CSB), **"And this is eternal life, that they may know You, the only true God, and Jesus Christ whom You have sent."**

Can you hear the Father's cry for you to know Him and not solely about Him? Can you see Jesus' sacrifice that you would know the Father?

Command Satan to be removed from your presence and ask the Lord if there's anything He desires to say to you regarding these things.

JANUARY 27

Knowing Me is Joy. You can't have the Joy of the LORD and not know Me.

We've established that it's impossible to know God without hearing Him. You have to have a relationship with Him to know Him. Added to that, have you ever noticed that every time you hear the voice of the Lord, it's exciting? It's exciting to hear Him talk – to know that the One who is above all is talking to you.

"Do not sorrow, for the joy of the LORD is your strength." (Nehemiah 8:10b NKJV)

How does knowing Him produce joy? Can you see how those who do not know Him do not have real joy?

Command Satan to be removed from your presence and ask the Lord if there's anything He desires to say to you regarding having joy in knowing Him.

JANUARY 28

To KNOW Me is to love Me.

God is love. Whoever lives in love lives in God, and God in him. (1 John 4:16b NIV)

Eternal life is knowing God. If God is love, then knowing God is knowing Love. This knowing is not an intellectual knowledge, but a heart knowledge. If you know God, and not just know about Him, you will love Him. It's impossible not to.

Try to think of anyone who really knows God, but doesn't love Him. You can't do it. If someone says they know God and says they don't love Him, they're lying. They don't really know Him if they don't love Him. He is love and He can't be separated from it. In fact, we can't really love outside of Him.

Command Satan to be removed from your presence and ask the Holy Spirit more about why it would be impossible to know Him and not love Him. Write down what you hear.

JANUARY 29

My Spirit loves you so much. He's gentle and He wants to know you.

Look at the fruit of the Holy Spirit:

... the fruit of the Spirit is love, joy, peace, patience, kindness, goodness, faithfulness, gentleness, and self-control... (Galatians 5:23 NIV)

Love and gentleness are part of the fruit of the Spirit. This truly is how the Holy Spirit operates. This is why when you are filled with the Holy Spirit and following Him, you will become loving and gentle as well. When you are surrendered to Him, you become like Him.

The Holy Spirit doesn't push Himself on anyone, but desires to be invited in. He is so kind and gentle. He will wait for an invitation to know you. Invite Him to know you right now.

Prayer – Holy Spirit, know me. Know me. And, I want to know You. Amen.

Command Satan to be removed from your presence and ask the Lord if there's anything He desires to say to you regarding these things.

January 30

Come to Me boldly. I will never turn you away.

Read: Hebrews 7:25   Hebrews 4:16

Do you think Jesus is ever hesitant to come before Father and speak with Him? Would Father ever turn Jesus away?

Now, if you are in Christ, Father looks at you and sees His Son. Therefore, if you come boldly to Father through Jesus, will He ever turn you away? Of course not. He wants to know you and to have you know Him intimately. He said that if He's given us Jesus, how will He not along with Him graciously give us all things? He's not going to turn you away, be mad at you, think you're bothering Him, or any other negative thing. So, come boldly!

Command Satan to be removed from your presence and ask the Lord if there's anything He desires to say to you regarding these things.

JANUARY 31

What is truth?

Read: John 14:6   John 14:17   John 8:32 NIV

There is no truth outside of Jesus. God never changes, for the Scriptures declare that Jesus Christ is the same yesterday, today, and forever. This means whatever "truth" may be found outside of Christ is subject to change. But when we look to Jesus for truth, we know that will never change.

Jesus said that the Spirit of truth would lead us into all truth. The Spirit of truth is the Holy Spirit, who is the Spirit of Christ. If we want to know truth, we look to Jesus.

If Jesus is the Truth, what does that mean? We'll go into it more tomorrow, but for today, ponder with the Holy Spirit what Truth is – Who He is.

Truth supersedes the facts.

Read: John 9:1-12 NKJV   Hebrews 11:1 NIV

Is the sun hot? It's a fact that the sun is hot. But could Jesus – the Truth – change the fact that the sun is hot?

If someone falls and breaks their leg bone, is it a fact that their leg is broken? Of course. But, can Jesus heal that person so that their leg is no longer broken?

We tend to think facts are truth, but they're really not because they're subject to change; they're subject to the truth. All the things we view as fact are subject to the truth. Take the blind man in John chapter 9. It's a fact that he was born blind. He could not see. But when he encountered Jesus, the truth changed the facts, and the man could see.

So we can see that having faith in the truth changes the facts.

Ponder the difference between facts and truth today with the Holy Spirit.

FEBRUARY 2

The reality is Christ.

Read: Colossians 2:17 NIV   John 10:17-18 NIV

This is a vision Kirk had on September 17, 2019:

I had been feeling beat up spiritually. I felt as though I had been in a battle and was wounded. The Lord took me in a vision and showed me that the thought that I'd been beat up spiritually was deception. Then Jesus swept his arm several times. Each time Jesus would sweep His arm, the reality changed in front of me. I would be in one place that looked real. Then I would be in another place, and that looked real. The reality kept changing. When Jesus was done, He asked me which of these were real. I didn't know and Jesus said, "Kirk, they're all real. I Am reality itself. Everything exists in Me and for Me. Nothing exists apart from Me. The sense of reality that you experience apart from Me is a lie." I said I didn't understand because it feels real. Jesus said, "I know. It felt real to Me in the garden before My death on the cross too. Can you see that now after the cross I have proven it to be deception? I have conquered the deception of death and suffering! As I have shown you, death is up to you. I would have never died if I had not willingly given up My Spirit. You too don't have to die by sickness or accident or anything else — only when Father says to give up your spirit." I replied, "Jesus, it seems like this world is just a simulation then, and the reality awaits us." He says, "You're seeing correctly."

Reality according to Jesus is Truth. Therefore, the facts are subject to the truth. Jesus is LORD. He is the Truth, and that's why all facts are subject to Him. Facts are not your lord. Jesus is.

Command the atmosphere clear around you and ask Jesus to show you His reality in your life, because that's the truth.

FEBRUARY 3

We live and move and have our being because He is Life.

Read: Acts 17:28   Colossians 1:15-18   John 6:54
        John 1:3-4

There is no life outside of Christ. There is no life except for Christ. Before you were born again, did you really live? You may have been breathing, doing activities, interacting with other people, even feeling enjoyment. But were you alive?

When Jesus said He is the Life, He meant it. There really is no life outside of Him. Outside of Him, we are subject to death, and never really live. In Him, we are subject to life, and never really die.

Having read the Scriptures and statements above, can you see now how it is true that we live and move and have our being because HE is Life?

Ponder this with the Holy Spirit today.

Die continually, or live forever?

Read: Matthew 25:46   John 17:3

We know that if we are in Christ, we will live forever. It has also been said that if we are not in Christ, we'll live forever in Hell. That's really not true. You will go to Hell if you're not in Christ, but it won't be to live. In Hell there is no life, but only death. In Hell, a person dies continually, over and over and over again.

Besides the eternal destination, living and dying are a choice you make every day. Read the following excerpt from a prophetic word given on June 27, 2019.

The darkness shall increase, but the Light shall increase more. Those whose focus is on the darkness shall be overcome by it, but those who walk in the Light shall never be in darkness. Therefore, set your face toward the Light and not toward the darkness! If you have died to the darkness, you will never die again! If not, there will be no end to the death you will die.

Dying to the darkness means dying to fear, what you think and feel. It's really dying to self. When you die to self, you've died to fear. In Hell, there is constant fear, constant death. So then, we make a choice. We can die once to self and fear, and so live in freedom. Or we can die day after day, and never really live.

Command the atmosphere clear and speak to the Holy Spirit about this.

FEBRUARY 5

No one has seen the Father.

Read: John 3:13   John 14:9   Hebrews 1:3
        Hebrews 10:19-20

If no one has seen the Father, but Jesus is the exact representation of the Father and even says that to see Him is to see the Father, how can we know the Father without Him? Jesus is the One who came down from Heaven, so He's the only One qualified to reveal the Father to us.

If Jesus, who is seated at the right hand of Father, sees Father and you're in Him, can you see Father?

Command the atmosphere clear and ask the Holy Spirit about this.

FEBRUARY 6

I Am your peace.

Read: Isaiah 9:6   Isaiah 53:5   John 14:27

The Prince of Peace has become peace for us. He paid for our peace through His body and blood. In Him, we have peace. Outside of Him, there is no peace. The One who calms the seas, casts out demons so that people are in their right minds, heals the sick, raises the dead back to life, and comforts the downcast, is the One who brings us peace. That peace is an everlasting peace. It is not as the world gives in any respect, but it is eternal. We only need to rest in Him, and we shall have His peace fill us.

Prayer: Jesus, I receive Your peace right now. I choose to believe You paid for my peace. Therefore, by faith, I receive it. Thank You! Amen.

I Am the Good Shepherd.

Read: John 10:11-15

A good shepherd gives his life for his sheep. Someone who's hired to work, will not do so.

Sometimes people say, "If God is good, why does this bad thing happen?" The question really is, "If God wasn't good, why would He send His Son to die for a bunch of sinners?" If Jesus wasn't good, why would He lay His life down for you when you were His enemy?

Colossians 1:21 says that we were alienated and enemies in our minds by wicked works before Christ redeemed us. We could only be made good by the One who is good. That Good Shepherd laid down His life. Is there anyone we can trust, more than Him? Is there anyone or anything or any system worthy of our trust more than Him? He's the Good Shepherd. He's the One who has laid down everything for us.

Ask the Holy Spirit to show you Jesus as the Good Shepherd today.

I Am always for you.

Read: Romans 8:28-32   Hebrews 7:25

God is for us and Jesus always lives to make intercession for us. If we are in Christ, there is no way God cannot be for us. We're in Christ and Father is definitely for Christ! And He is always for you. If He's not giving you what He's promised to you right now, it doesn't mean He's not for you. He works all things for the good of those who love Him. That's **all things**! If it's not good yet, He's not done yet.

Rejoice, God is always for you!

Prayer: Father, I thank You that You are always for me. I am in Your Son, and I know You are always for Your Son. I trust You! Amen.

FEBRUARY 9

I Am never against you.

Read: Romans 8:33-39

Yesterday we saw that God is always for us. Well, the other side of that, is that He is **never** against us. How could He be against His own Son? And are you not *in* His Son? There is absolutely nothing that can separate you from His love for He is Love; and you are in Him and He is in you.

The liar says that God is mad at you, or God doesn't love you, or God is working against you. The blood of Jesus says that's a lie. He shed His blood to make peace between you and your Father. That blood lives forever! Don't believe the lie that God is against you. He is for you when you are in His Son. God is Love and Love never fails! Believe God!

Command the enemy to be silent and ask the Holy Spirit about this.

I Am never the accuser.

Read: Zechariah 3:1-2   (NIV) Revelation 12:10
Hebrews 10:22 (NIV)

The accuser of the brethren is the devil. He will speak through others many times, but it's the accuser just the same. The Lord Jesus Christ never accuses you. He paid the price for you to be saved. He paid for you to be free from accusation. The devil can accuse all day long, but not one accusation will stick to the righteous, for we are in Christ.

If God accused you, what good would the sacrifice of Jesus be? It would be worthless. Jesus not only paid for your sin, but He cleanses the guilty conscience. You are truly set free! If you hear that accusing voice, tell it to get behind you, for you are **not** accused! It's what God says that matters, not the liar.

Prayer: Father, I thank You that You never accuse me. Jesus, You never accuse me. Holy Spirit, You never accuse me. I am accepted and loved and righteous! Thank You! Amen.

FEBRUARY 11

No one can come to the Father, except by Me.

Read: John 14:6   John 1:18

Jesus came to destroy the works of the devil; that's true. He became sin for us; that's true. He came to show us how to live as a man filled with the Holy Spirit; that's true. But what it's all summed up in, is that Jesus came to reveal the Father to us. He came to reconcile us to our Father.

Jesus came down from Heaven and humbled Himself to actually become what He had created – a man, so that we could be reconciled to our Father, so that we could actually know our Father! Jesus said, **"And this is eternal life, that they may know You, the only true God, and Jesus Christ whom You have sent."** (John 17:3)

The Father was pleased to reveal Himself through His Son, and it is through His Son that we may know Him. There is no other way. When Jesus said He was the Way, that's what He meant. He didn't mean He was a way to Father, but the way to Father. It requires humility on our part because we have to admit we've fallen short and can't reach Father on our own. We need to die and live again in Christ, that we may be reconciled to our Father. That's the only way.

Praise You, Jesus! You are the Way!

I and the Father are One.

Read: John 10:30   John 14:9

'*Believe Me when I tell you that My Father and I are One. If I love you, then My Father loves you. If My Father loves you, then I love You. We are not separate, but One. Our love for you will not end or run out, or even wane. Look to Me and see Your Father. There is no distinction. Therefore, when you speak to Me, you speak to My Father. When you speak to Father, you speak to Me. When you hear Father speaking, you're hearing Me. When you hear Me, you hear the Father."*

Therefore, do not let confusion reign, but remember that the Father and the Son do not have differing opinions. They are One.

Wherever I Am, there is Light.

Read: John 8:12   John 3:19   John 12:46

Are you born again? Does Jesus live in you? He is the Light of the world. If He is in you, then that light shines through you. Wherever He is, there is light. The darkness leaves when the Light arrives. Darkness only remains where there is no light.

Jesus said in Matthew 5:16, **"Let your light so shine before men, that they may see your good works and glorify your Father in heaven."** So, what is that light you're supposed to shine? It is Jesus. He is the light that you allow to shine and that brings glory to Father. And how do you allow Him to shine? Through your good works. But remember, those are the good works God prepared in advance for you to do. They're the works you do as led by the Holy Spirit. They are not the works that you think are good or that religion decides are good for you to do. It's all by following that the Light shines. And you do shine, for wherever Jesus is, there is Light!

FEBRUARY 14

I Am the LORD.

Read: Revelation 17:14   Revelation 19:16
        Isaiah 45:18

To be LORD means to rule and reign. Whatever you make lord is what rules in your life. Are your feelings lord? Are your circumstances lord? Are sports lord? How about money? How about food or drugs? How about self? The list could go on.

However, we know who is LORD. There is only One and His name is Jesus. He is the LORD and there is no other. He rules supreme and though the nations rage and people plot against Him, it's all in vain, for as the Scriptures testify: **"[T]hat at the name of Jesus every knee should bow, of those in Heaven, and of those on Earth, and of those under the earth…"**. (Philippians 2:10)

To bow our knee to Him means that we agree with Him in all things. If He is LORD, then what He says goes. It's His way, and not another.

Praise You Jesus – You are LORD!

I do NOT grow weary.

Read: Isaiah 40:28-31

Have you ever considered that God doesn't ever get tired? He doesn't grow weary, physically, or emotionally, or spiritually. So what does that mean for us?

The passage in Isaiah 40 tells us that He neither faints nor grows weary and that He gives strength to the weak, so that they have renewed strength. They are able to run and not be weary, they are able to walk and not faint, etc. Sounds like God's strength, doesn't it?

What's the prerequisite for us to receive that kind of strength? The Scripture says, "Those who wait on the Lord…". The word "wait" in Hebrew means to wait, look for, hope, or expect. And the Scriptures further testify in Hebrews that faith is being sure of what we hope for and certain of what we do not see. (Hebrews 1:1 NIV) Therefore, those who wait on the Lord are those who are hoping for, expecting, the promised things to come to pass. As they wait, or as they believe the Lord, their strength is renewed and like God, they shall not grow weary or faint; we could even say they won't become faint-hearted.

Our God does not grow weary, and we too shall not grow weary as we wait on Him. Amen.

I do not change.

Read: Hebrews 13:8   Malachi 3:6(a)

A thing is established on the testimony of two or three witnesses. Well, what we just read are two witnesses that God does not change, and in fact, He is the same as He always was and always will be.

Therefore, do not let the devil deceive you into believing that God is somehow different than He used to be or that He will be different in the future. How He is, is how He was and how He will always be. And if you want to know how He is, was, and will be, look to the Son because He is the *exact* representation of the Father. If you don't see it in Jesus, then it shouldn't be in your theology.

Rest in the truth that God does not change. He is dependable to be a good Father, a worthy Savior, a Holy Lord, the Way, the Truth, the Life, your Great Defender and Deliverer, an Ever-Present Help in time of trouble, the One who leads you into all truth and makes you holy, the One who always lives to make intercession for us, the One who holds the keys to life and death, the Just Judge, the Word of God, the One who is Love, and the list goes on.

Everyone and everything around us may change, but God never will.

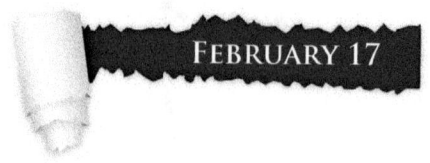

FEBRUARY 17

I Am the great <u>I AM</u>!

Read: Exodus 3:13-15   John 8:54-58   John 18:4-6 (Actually reads "I Am", not "I Am He")

What does it mean that God is I Am? Do not the Scriptures testify that Jesus is the Life? Doesn't Colossians 1:16-17 say, **"For by Him all things were created that are in heaven and that are on earth, visible and invisible, whether thrones or dominions or principalities or powers. All things were created through Him and for Him. And He is before all things, and in Him all things consist."**?

If He Himself is Life and there is no life outside of Him, for He says that eternal life is to know God and Jesus Christ whom He has sent, then for God to call Himself the Great I Am is accurate. For to be alive is to be in Him. We all have eternal spirits, but those not in Christ will die eternally, not live eternally. All life is in Him because He is I AM. He is the Great I AM!

Is there something God could call Himself that would be greater than I AM? For in that name, we see that He is all in all. He is Life itself. There is no life outside of Him. Is it any wonder that Jesus called Himself I AM? For Jesus is the Way, the Truth, and the Life. There's no other way to Father except through Him, the I AM.

FEBRUARY 18

James 2:19 You believe that there is one God. Good! Even the demons believe that – and shudder!

(NIV for all Scriptures today.)

Read: Deuteronomy 6:4   Mark 12:29   John 14:9
        Hebrews 1:3   John 17:3

Theology means the study of God. Many people study God. Many people know a lot about God. Many people can quote Scriptures and argue points about God really well. They would agree that there is one God and argue that point well.

However, the last Scripture we read for today's devotional says that eternal life is to know God and Jesus Christ, whom He has sent. Is knowing about God the same as knowing God? Is knowing God is One, the same as knowing the God who is One?

James testifies that even the demons know there is one God – and shudder at the very thought. The demons are well aware God is One, and Satan himself can quote Scripture probably better than any man. So, knowing about God and knowing God are evidently different.

Therefore, even testifying that Jesus is God, and the Holy Spirit is God – meaning God is One – does not mean that you actually know God. Knowing God is salvation, and Jesus came that we may know God. Jesus came not merely to save you and change your eternal destination. He made you into His image – born again and filled with the very Spirit of the Living God who raised Him from the dead and now raises you from death, as well!

Prayer: Holy Spirit, we want to know You! We want to know our Father! We want to know our Lord Jesus! We want You! Come Holy Spirit and give us knowing today! Amen.

FEBRUARY 19

Theology is Jesus

Read: Hebrews 1:1-3 (NIV) John 1:18 (NKJV)

If you want to study God, study Jesus. Jesus is the exact representation of God. "If you've seen Me, you've seen the Father," Jesus told Philip.

Father and Jesus are One. So, if we want to know Father, we do that through the Son. Jesus is the One who declares Father to us. Jesus is the One who came from Heaven and ascended back there. Jesus is the One who sent us His Spirit that we may know Him and our Father in Heaven. Jesus is the One to Whom Father has given all things and now those things are declared to us by His Spirit.

Therefore, Jesus Christ is perfect theology. If we want to know God, we look to the Son. Whatever the Son says, whatever the Son does, whatever the Son believes, that's what God is saying, doing, and believing. So that is what we say, do, and believe. too.

Could you hear God's voice if He was offending your theology?

Read: John 6:53-63

Jesus is perfect theology, right? That's what we learned yesterday. Yet, He's called a stone of stumbling and a rock of offense in the Scriptures. This is because He is the only way. Our thoughts about God can really be offended in Him.

Look at the Scripture reading for today. He was telling His disciples to eat His flesh and drink His blood. They got offended. So, He told them He was going away. Well, that's even more offensive because they thought He was coming to set up an earthly kingdom, right then.

Sometimes what we've learned about God gets offended when presented with the Truth – Jesus. Don't let this offense have any say in whether you believe God or not. Many of Jesus' disciples left Him after that passage in John 6. But those close to Him stayed even though they didn't understand, because as Peter said in verse 68, "Lord, to whom shall we go? You have the words of eternal life." In other words, "We don't get it, but we know what You speak is true, so we're going to believe You."

Do this with God when what is revealed is offensive to you. Tell Him you trust Him and you're going to believe Him anyway, regardless of how offensive it is.

Why is Jesus considered our Healer, and we don't really consider Jehovah Rapha?

Read: Exodus 15:26   Psalm 103:3   Ephesians 1:19-21
Acts 4:7-10

God has many names. One of those names revealed in the Old Covenant is Jehovah Rapha – God, our Healer. Yet, when we lay hands on someone for healing and command sickness to leave them, we do it in the name of Jesus and not in the name of Jehovah Rapha. Why? Is this right?

Because we pray and command things to happen in the name of Jesus doesn't mean that God has changed His name. It means Jesus is the summation of the names of God. He is the Healer. He is the Deliverer. His is the Name above every name. When we speak the name of Jesus, we speak that God is our Healer, that God is our Salvation, that God is our Deliverer. There is no higher name, for He is seated at the right hand of the Father, far above every name that is named.

God has always made a way for healing because He is good. He didn't bring sickness and sin into the world. The devil is the one who comes to steal, to kill, and to destroy. So, even under the Old Covenant, we see God healing people. But there is a stark contrast between the Old Covenant and the New Covenant. Now it's not that people need to encounter a prophet to be healed. Healing is for everyone through Christ Jesus. He became sin for us, and He took the stripes for our healing. By faith in Him, we are healed.

Prayer: Praise You, Father that we see You, Jehovah Rapha, in Your Son, Christ Jesus! Amen!

FEBRUARY 22

Did Jesus do the healing, or was it the Spirit working through Him?

Read: Matthew 3:16   Matthew 4:23-24   Luke 4:18
       Luke 5:17

We started our reading today with the baptism of Jesus. Then we saw what happened after His baptism. Have you ever noticed that before Jesus was baptized and the Spirit of God came upon Him, He didn't perform any miracles? It was only after the Holy Spirit came upon Him that He performed miracles, healed the sick, and cast out devils.

The Holy Spirit is the power of God. Jesus humbled Himself to become a Man and waited to be filled with the power of God before He began healing and doing miracles. It's obvious that the same is true for His followers today. Those who are filled with the Spirit of God, do the works of God. Those who are not, do not.

The Holy Spirit lifted up Jesus by working through Him, and He still lifts up Jesus by working through those of us who carry His name.

Prayer: Holy Spirit, praise You for working through me. I surrender to You.

FEBRUARY 23

What part did the Father play in Jesus' ministry?

Read: John 5:16-23   John 14:8-11

Jesus didn't do anything He didn't see Father doing and didn't speak anything He didn't hear Father saying. The works Jesus did testified that He was one with His Father. Therefore, He could say to Philip that if he had seen Jesus, he had seen the Father.

The ministry Jesus did He got from His Father. He saw what His Father was doing, and He did that. He heard what His Father was saying, and He spoke that. That is how His words were Spirit and Life. They came from His Father; the Spirit of God brought them to Jesus. The source of power came from the Father, for it is the Father who sent His Spirit to His Son.

Now Jesus says that we who believe in Him will do what He has done and greater because He goes to His Father and sends us His Spirit. When we do ministry in the name of Jesus, the Father is glorified in the Son. (John 14:12-14)

Prayer: Father, we praise You for sending Your Son. We praise You for the gift of Your Spirit. Be glorified in Your Son! Amen.

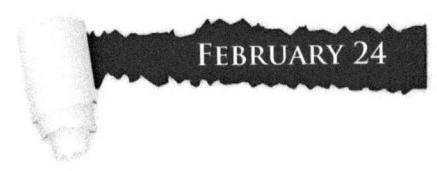

FEBRUARY 24

What is the difference between knowing God and knowing about Him?

Read: John 9:29   John 5:38-47   John 17:3

Theology is the study of God. The Pharisees of Jesus' day and the theologians of today spend a great amount of time studying God. Yet, what did Jesus tell the Pharisees and teachers of the Law?

He told them that though they search the Scriptures, they don't know Him because they're not willing to come to Him. They weren't willing to lay down what they believed to be true in order to have the truth.

Eternal life is to know God. Knowing about God will never be enough. James says that even the demons believe there is One God and shudder! Knowing something about someone and actually knowing someone are totally different.

Therefore, don't be impressed with great knowledge about God. Be impressed with those who actually walk with Him. That's what you want to be emulating. Knowledge puffs up, but love builds up! (1 Corinthians 8:1)

FEBRUARY 25

Should we study Judaism since Jesus railed against the Pharisees and the Law?

Read: Philippians 3:1-11   Colossians 2:2b-3

Is it necessary to know all the background of Judaism and Israel in order to know God? Do those who have this knowledge have an advantage over those who don't?

Paul was a great example of a "Jew's Jew," and yet what did he say about all that knowledge or all that perfect lineage? He counted it as nothing! It's nothing in Christ! In Christ is all that matters.

Therefore, where is all wisdom and knowledge found? It is "hidden in Christ," means that it is found in Christ. All wisdom and all knowledge is found in Christ. Outside of Christ, there's nothing that matters.

Does this make the study of Judaism bad then? Well, that depends. Has the Holy Spirit told you to study Judaism? If so, go ahead and ask Him for revelation as you study. The problem lies in trying to gain some knowledge outside of Christ that we think we need in order to understand something.

Judaism, like other religions, isn't going to save anyone. Salvation is found in Christ alone. Wisdom is found in Christ alone. Look to Him for what you need. As Paul writes in 1 Corinthians 1:30, Jesus became wisdom for us. Therefore, seek Him.

BAPTISM

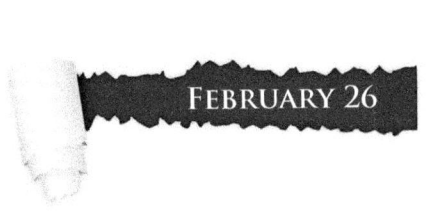
FEBRUARY 26

Seeing the Kingdom.

Read: John 3:3

Have you ever wondered why those around you who have not been born again cannot seem to see what's going on in the spirit? For instance, there may be a miraculous healing and the person unable to see will say something like, "Well, I guess the doctors were wrong." When all the while, you know the person was miraculously healed by the Lord!

Sometimes, there are events in the earth that are obviously happening by the hand of God, but those around you cannot seem to see it. You may see the significance of the rising and falling of leaders in the world, or the significance of events in nature, or the significance of court judgments, etc., but those around you don't get it.

Well, they cannot see the kingdom of God unless they are born again. It's really that simple. The Kingdom of God is Spirit and without the Spirit, there's no ability to see. Therefore, the necessity of being born again cannot be overstated. We cannot even see clearly without it. Our eyes are blinded without being born into Christ.

If you are not born again, and would like to give your life to Jesus and make Him Lord, then go ahead and pray the following prayer:

Jesus, I give You my life. I repent of my wicked ways and wicked thoughts. I want You to make me new. I want to follow You and live for You and not for myself anymore. Please fill me with Your Spirit and bring me to Father. I want to know Him and You and the Holy Spirit. Amen

Now, be filled with the Holy Spirit and be baptized in water! Congratulations!

FEBRUARY 27

Entering the Kingdom.

Read: John 3:5-7   Matthew 11:11

Without being born again and filled with the Spirit of God, you cannot enter the Kingdom of God. God is Spirit, and you must be born of the Spirit to be in His Kingdom. As Jesus testified about John the Baptist, John was the greatest man born of a woman, but those born again are greater. They are born of the water and the Spirit. They are born into Christ.

The necessity of entering God's Kingdom cannot be overstated. By faith, we gain access into Christ by His Spirit. The door is Jesus, the way is Jesus, the King in the Kingdom is Jesus. Enter through Him.

There's nothing hard about entering the Kingdom. The hard part is giving up what you think.

How can you know you're saved?

Read: 1 John 3:24   1 John 4:13

You know you are saved by the Spirit within you. Does the Holy Spirit abide in you? Do you know Him? Do you hear Him and have fellowship with Him? We know we are saved because of the witness of the Holy Spirit within us.

You cannot have assurance of salvation apart from the Holy Spirit. It's really that simple.

We (Kirk & Tiffany) were both raised in church, all of our lives. In a similar way, we lived for the flesh, though intellectually we knew the truth. However, there was never any real change in our lives. We'd pray regularly to be forgiven and saved, but we never really had any assurance that we were. That all changed with the baptism of the Holy Spirit.

John the Baptist testified that he baptized with water, but Jesus would baptize with the Holy Spirit. Water is natural. The Holy Spirit is supernatural. Water in and of itself cannot change anything, but the outside, making the outside of a person clean. The Holy Spirit has the power to change the inside. "From the fullness of His glory, we have received grace upon grace!" (John 1:16)

Once you've received the fullness of the Holy Spirit, you know the grace of God is in you and on you. You start to change on the outside because of the changes He brings on the inside. You begin to know

His voice, and as you follow Him, you know Him more and more intimately. No one should be able to convince you that you are not saved when you are filled with the Holy Spirit; because He bears witness that Christ is in you.

Without the Holy Spirit, you cannot have that assurance. It is by the Holy Spirit that you know you are saved.

MARCH 1

Can you be saved and not have the Holy Spirit?

Read: Romans 8:9   1 John 3:24

Yesterday, we discussed how it is the witness of the Holy Spirit in you that assures you of your salvation. So, what happens if you don't have the Holy Spirit? Well, Paul testifies that if you don't have the Spirit, you do not belong to Christ. It seems pretty self-explanatory.

The problem is that we want to know the bare minimum we need to get by. What's the least we have to do to be saved? But the Holy Spirit says, *"I Am God. You either receive Me, or you don't."*

If you are in Christ, you know it by His Spirit. If you do not have the Spirit of Christ, you are not in Him. That's what Father is saying. The Lord is saying to choose. Choose Jesus or choose self. If you choose Jesus, then you want His Spirit too.

Praise God for His Holy Spirit!

March 2

If you're baptized in the Holy Spirit, do you always have the gift of tongues?

Read: Acts 2:1-4   Acts 10:44-48   Acts 19:1-6
Romans 8:32

The Holy Spirit desires to give us His gifts. When people are baptized in the Holy Spirit, they do receive tongues, as evidenced by the Scriptures we read and many others.

Don't look for reasons to disbelieve, instead look for the opportunity to have faith. The Holy Spirit says, "Have faith that I come with tongues!"

Every gift comes by faith. Which means you can be baptized in the Holy Spirit and not have faith for tongues. If you have faith, will it be withheld? No, because all things are possible to those who believe. The Lord wants you to believe.

If you've been baptized in the Holy Spirit and haven't prayed in tongues yet, then open your mouth and as you pray .Start speaking in faith, but not in your native language.

Prayer: Holy Spirit, even as you have filled this child of God, so now speak through them with the gift of tongues!

MARCH 3

Can you prophesy if you're filled with the Holy Spirit?

Read: John 16:13   Revelation 19:10

Jesus said the Holy Spirit would tell you things to come, so if you have the Holy Spirit, you expect to prophesy. Additionally, the testimony of Jesus is the Spirit of prophecy, so as you give testimony of what you have seen and heard – testimony of Jesus – you are prophesying. You are saying, "God, do it again!"

Therefore, not only can you prophesy if you're filled with the Holy Spirit, but you will!

Paul writes in 1 Corinthians 14:1 to eagerly desire the spiritual gifts, but especially that you may prophesy. So, pursue it! Ask the Holy Spirit to tell you things to come, as Jesus said He would do. When you look at people, ask the Holy Spirit to show you what is to come in their lives and then in boldness, speak it over them! It will be a testimony to them and release power in their lives for the word of God to come to pass.

This is the greatest gift, so go after it with your whole heart!

MARCH 4

Why is the Holy Spirit called "the Spirit of Christ" in the Scriptures?

Read: Romans 8:9   1 Peter 1:10-11   Galatians 4:6-7

In the same passage we see that Paul calls the Spirit of God the Spirit of Christ. The names are interchangeable. He is referring to the Holy Spirit, as Peter does in his letter.

When we get to Galatians 4, Paul tells us that God has sent the Spirit of His Son into our hearts, making us sons. We understand that it is the Holy Spirit to Whom he is referring. We cannot be a son without the Holy Spirit in us, for we cannot be holy without the Holy Spirit. And how could God call us sons without first making us holy?

Paul also writes in Galatians 3:26-27 (NKJV), **"For you are all sons of God through faith in Christ Jesus. For as many of you as were baptized into Christ have put on Christ."**

Our baptism into Christ is not complete without the Holy Spirit. Therefore, to be one with Christ, we need His Spirit and that Spirit is the Holy Spirit.

Today, praise Jesus for His Spirit – the Holy Spirit of God. Praise Father for making us sons through His Son and His Spirit. And praise the Holy Spirit for agreeing to live in you, making you holy!

MARCH 5

Have you been baptized in the Holy Spirit?

Read: Acts 19:1-6 (NKJV)   Matthew 3:16

Can you separate water and Holy Spirit baptism? Can you separate God (Father, Son, and Holy Spirit)? Why would believing in Jesus and not receiving His Holy Spirit be incomplete?

Command Satan to be removed from your presence and ask the Lord if there's anything He desires to say to you regarding these things. Look up 1 Corinthians 12:13 (NIV) and ponder with the Holy Spirit these scriptures and questions.

MARCH 6

Continue to press in regarding the baptism of Jesus, My Son. My Spirit will lead you into all truth.

Read: Ephesians 4:4-6

There's one baptism, yet there's three mentioned in Scripture: water, fire, and Holy Spirit. There's One God, yet Father, Son, and Holy Spirit are clearly identified in Scripture. What relationship do you see between One God and one baptism? Can they be separate? Can you see why Hebrews 6:1-2 mentions the word "baptisms"? Yet, can it be one? Can your baptism into Christ be complete with part or one of them done?

Command Satan to be removed from your presence and ask the Lord if there's anything He desires to say to you regarding these things.

Baptism of the Holy Spirit.

Read: Acts 7:51 (NKJV)

It should be obvious by now that Jesus wants to fill you with His Spirit. He says His Spirit will fall on all who are willing to carry Him.

Would you like to resist no more? Lift up your hands and ask Jesus to baptize you in His Holy Spirit! Today is your day!

Jesus, we pray in agreement for you to baptize your child in your Holy Spirit, enduing them with power from on high! Thank You, Amen!

MARCH 8

Fire fall!

Read: Acts 2:36-39, 41   Acts 17:6

After Jesus was crucified, and before they were baptized in the Holy Spirit and fire, the disciples went fishing. They caught nothing. (John 21:3)

After they were baptized in the Holy Spirit and fire, they changed the world. It takes fire to change the world.

The Lord, Jesus, desires His fire to fall on you in the same way it fell on the earlier disciples. Let the desire for fire burn in you today.

Pray for the desire for the baptism in fire.

Burn Hot!

Read: Luke 12:49   Acts 1:8

Jesus desires us to burn with the fire from God. With the outpouring of the Holy Spirit, comes also the baptism of fire. This fire completes your baptism into Christ. Through water, fire, and the Holy Spirit, you are born again with a good heart, filled with power, and filled with fire.

Pray to receive the baptism of fire today! Then go and spread the fire of the gospel of Jesus Christ in power!

MARCH 10

Why would you want the baptism of the Holy Spirit?

Read: Philippians 1:21   Acts 1:4-5

What do you want to get out of being a Christian? Is your desire simply to get to Heaven? Do you desire health and prosperity, perhaps; or do you desire to be like Christ? Do you want Him to live through you, and the old you to be buried in the grave? Do you desire to be perfect, even as He is perfect? Do you desire His gifts and power to flow through you to those around you?

If your desire is the same as Paul testified, "For me to live is Christ," then you desire the Holy Spirit. It's impossible to be like Christ without His Spirit.

Jesus testifies that the Holy Spirit is the promise from the Father. God in us! Really, if you're a disciple of Jesus, why wouldn't you want the baptism of the Holy Spirit? There's every good reason to want Him, and no good reason to not want Him! In fact, the Holy Spirit is God. If you don't want Him, you don't want God.

If you don't have the Holy Spirit, ask Jesus to baptize you in His Spirit today!

March 11

What does it do for a person to have the baptism of the Holy Spirit?

Read: Acts 1:8   John 15:26   John 16:13
        1 Corinthians 12:4 & 11

The benefits of being baptized in the Holy Spirit are too much to discuss in a short devotional, if we were even able to list or understand them all!

However, from the Scripture reading today, we can see some benefits of being baptized in the Holy Spirit. He is the power sent from God. He is the One who leads us into all truth and brings us what Jesus says. He is the Helper and the Comforter.

The Holy Spirit is also the one who disperses His gifts. These gifts help build up the body of Christ and prove God true to unbelievers.

Beyond this, the Holy Spirit comes to dwell inside of us. This means God never leaves us. He is always with us. We become partakers of His divine nature through His Spirit that dwells in us. The very life of Christ fills our mortal bodies through His Spirit that lives in us. He conforms us into the image of Jesus!

Today, reflect with the Holy Spirit on what it does for you to have Him living in you.

MARCH 12

When should children be baptized?

Read: Acts 16:25-34

In this bit of history, we see that a whole household put their faith in Jesus Christ and were baptized. The Scriptures say the jailer believed in God "with all his household." That would include children.

The only prerequisite to baptism is faith. When someone believes, there is action because faith without works is dead (James 2:17). That action is a repentant heart. This means anyone of any age that believes with their heart can be saved, and therefore, baptized.

As we've learned before, the baptism into Christ includes the whole thing – water, Spirit, and fire. When a child desires this, don't hold them back. They need the Holy Spirit as much as an adult. They need to be born again just as much as an adult. Whenever the Spirit moves on their hearts, don't hinder them, but allow them to come to Him.

However, don't force it. You cannot force someone to be born again. It has to come from their heart. In other words, you can't baptize them into Christ unless they've believed and are born again. Anything you do against their will, will not work.

Prayer: Holy Spirit, move on our children's hearts today! Father, draw them to You in the name of Your Son, Jesus! Jesus, we exalt You! Fill our children with Your Spirit and fire as they believe in You. Amen!

HOLY SPIRIT

Watch for My Spirit to move today.

Read: Isaiah 61:1   2 Corinthians 3:17

Jesus has come to break the chains of bondage and bring people into the freedom of the Spirit of the LORD. Where the Spirit of the LORD is, there is freedom. Jesus says in Luke 4:21, **"Today this Scripture is fulfilled in your hearing."**

Therefore, watch for the Holy Spirit to move today. Surely there will be freedom. Amen.

March 14

"Blessed shall you be when you come in, and blessed shall you be when you go out."

Read: Deuteronomy 28:6 (above)   Ephesians 1:3

We have been blessed with every spiritual blessing in Christ Jesus. Every spiritual blessing. The Lord is saying that we have entered the time of blessing.

Remember the cost of discipleship? Jesus said, *"Assuredly, I say to you, there is no one who has left house or brothers or sisters or father or mother or wife or children or lands, for My sake and the gospel's, who shall not receive a hundredfold now in this time -houses and brothers and sisters and mothers and children and lands, with persecutions – and in the age to come eternal life."*

The Lord says, "It is time." It is time to be blessed when you come in and blessed when you go out. Give thanks to the LORD for He is good! (See Psalm 107.)

MARCH 15

Yield to the wind of the Spirit.

Romans 8:1 NKJV **There is therefore now no condemnation to those who are in Christ Jesus, who do not walk according to the flesh, but according to the Spirit.**

Romans 8:14 NKJV **For as many as are led by the Spirit of God, these are the sons of God.**

The Lord asks, *"Is it easier to walk against the wind or to walk with the wind at your back? It is easier to walk with the wind at your back, isn't it? In like manner, it is easier to walk with My Spirit, yielding to Him. If you want to walk with Me, you must yield to My Spirit. My ways of doing things are not the ways of the world. Do you want this adventure of yielding to My Spirit? Turn around. Quit resisting and yield to My Spirit today."*

Command the enemy to be silent and tell the Holy Spirit you yield to His wind today, right now. Listen for His answer to you.

MARCH 16

The Wind of the Spirit always leads to...?

Read: John 16:15 (NIV)

Who does the Holy Spirit always glorify? (Read John 16:14)

Whose authority does Holy Spirit always speak on; Who does He hear from? (Read John 16:13)

Everything is about Jesus. Jesus is who Father is interested in. So, it's not strange that the Holy Spirit glorifies Jesus and always speaks what He hears from Jesus. One of the things Holy Spirit does is He leads us into all truth. Who is the Truth? Jesus. Yes, it's all about Jesus.

Command the enemy to be quiet and ask the Holy Spirit to speak to you regarding these things.

March 17

Jesus is My exact representation.

Read: Hebrews 1:1-3   John 15:26   Revelation 19:10

Jesus is the exact representation of Father, or the "express image" of Him. This means if we want to know what God is like, we look at Jesus.

We also know that the Holy Spirit testifies of Jesus. He is the Spirit of Christ. And we overcome the enemy by the blood of the Lamb and the word of our testimony; and loving our lives not unto death. The word of our testimony is the testimony of Jesus brought to us by the Holy Spirit. If you're a Christian, you carry the Holy Spirit who testifies of Jesus. This is the same Jesus who is the express image of God.

So, now you represent God through the Spirit of Christ who dwells in you. That's powerful!

Command Satan to be removed from your presence and ask the Lord if there's anything He desires to say to you regarding these things.

MARCH 18

Jesus has sent you the Promised Holy Spirit.

Read: John 16:7 (NIV)   John 10:30   John 17:11   John 17:21

Jesus said that it was for our good that He went away so that the Holy Spirit could come to us. That's incredible! We may wonder sometimes why it is better for Him to have left so that Holy Spirit could come.

But, have you ever considered how you can be one with Jesus and Father if you didn't have the Holy Spirit? It's by His Spirit that we can be one with Him. It's by His Spirit that we know Him. It's by His Spirit that we're changed into His image. And so much more...

Command Satan to be removed from your presence and ask the Lord if there's anything He desires to say to you regarding these things.

MARCH 19

The Holy Spirit and power.

Read: Acts 1:4-5 & 8   Acts 2:1-4   Acts 10:38
        Matthew 12:28

Jesus told His disciples to wait for the promised Holy Spirit before they went out to bring the message of the Kingdom. Jesus, Himself, waited for the power of the Holy Spirit before He began His ministry. In fact, Jesus did everything He did by the Spirit of God.

Do we believe we can operate without the power of the Holy Spirit? If we're doing things in our own strength, who gets the glory? And who's work are we really doing? If it's God's works, won't it take God's power? And if Jesus needed the Holy Spirit to do the works of God, wouldn't we need Him too?

Command Satan to be removed from your presence and ask the Lord if there's anything He desires to say to you regarding these things.

MARCH 20

The Holy Spirit is the Spirit of Christ.

Read: John 7:38-39   Philippians 1:19   John 15:26

The Holy Spirit is Christ in the world, because He is the Spirit of Christ. He glorifies Jesus, bringing us what is Jesus – the Truth. Therefore, He leads us into all truth.

The Holy Spirit also conforms us into the image of our Lord and Savior. It is only by the power of the Holy Spirit that we can be made like Christ. There's no other way.

Because the Holy Spirit is the Spirit of Christ, Jesus is the One who is the baptizer of the Holy Spirit. It is His Spirit He pours out on those who belong to him. To be in Christ, is to have His Spirit and follow Him.

Why is it better that Jesus left?

Read: John 16:7   Acts 1:5 & 8

Have you ever wished Jesus was physically right here so you could ask Him your questions? Or, so you could get to know Him? Or, so He could reach out His hand and heal you?

Do you understand that the same Spirit that raised Jesus from the dead lives in you when you are born again? (Romans 8:11) This is the same Spirit that came upon Jesus when He was baptized by John (Matthew 3:16). Jesus did all that He did through the power of the Holy Spirit.

Now, He sends that same Spirit to those of us who believe. This is the Spirit who Jesus said would bring to us everything that He says (John 14:26). Therefore, if you have a question, ask! The Holy Spirit is right there with you to answer. If you want to know Christ, you know Him through His Spirit. If you need healing, it's available to you through the Spirit of Christ.

It is better that Jesus went away because instead of needing to be near Him in the physical realm, we are able to be with Him constantly because His Spirit lives in us, and never leaves us or forsakes us. His power, His voice, His comfort, His authority is always with us through His Spirit who dwells in us!

Prayer: Thank You Jesus for giving us Your Holy Spirit! Thank You Holy Spirit for agreeing to live in us! Hallelujah! Amen.

What does it mean to blaspheme the Holy Spirit?

Read: Matthew 12:31   Mark 3:28-30   Luke 12:10
Hebrews 6:4-6   Hebrews 10:26-29

The American Heritage Dictionary defines "insult" as "to treat with gross insensitivity, insolence, or contemptuous rudeness; to affront or demean; or to make an attack on."

When we consider the Scriptures we read, we can see that insulting the Spirit of Grace is something more than unknowingly calling what is of God "from the devil." Paul called the things of God, of the devil. He said he was forgiven because of his ignorance and unbelief (1 Timothy 1:13).

Blaspheming the Holy Spirit is something that is knowingly done. You don't accidently blaspheme. A blasphemer of the Holy Spirit is one who is knowingly calling those things of the Spirit of God "of the devil." They purposely do it, knowing what they're doing.

MARCH 23

Shoes come with tongues. So does the Holy Spirit.

Read: Acts 2:3-4 NKJV   Acts 19:6   Acts 10:44-48

How did these people in your reading know they received the Holy Spirit? They spoke in tongues and prophesied. The Holy Spirit desires you to speak in tongues. Praying in tongues edifies you, and it's something you can do anytime, anywhere because you don't have to be loud about it. And the Scriptures testify that when tongues are interpreted, it holds the same weight as prophecy. That's pretty amazing because prophecy is the greatest gift.

Additionally, have you ever noticed that the greater things are always opposed the most heavily by the enemy? Tongues are definitely opposed in the church. They are ridiculed and talked down about. That alone should make you desire them!

Ask the Holy Spirit to give you tongues, if you do not already pray in tongues. Then by faith, open your mouth and start praying aloud. You can also start singing aloud in tongues! It may sound really weird to you, but don't give up!

Is the Holy Spirit a person?

Read: John 14:26   John 15:26   Romans 8:26
      1 Corinthians 12:11   Matthew 28:19

If you haven't figured it out from the Scriptures we read, yes, the Holy Spirit is a person. In Matthew 28, Jesus puts Him in the same sentence as He puts Himself and Father.

The Holy Spirit speaks, He leads, He intercedes, He comforts, He guides, He empowers, He makes holy, He brings us what Jesus is saying, and much more.

He is not some force somewhere that only affects things. He is God. Just as you are a body, soul, and spirit and are not really complete without the whole package, so God is Father, Son, and Spirit. They are One.

Therefore, when you pray, when you listen, treat the Holy Spirit as a person. He is Love. He is God. He is the Spirit of Christ living in you. Honor Him and love Him.

What does "the manifest presence" of the Holy Spirit mean?

Read: Matthew 3:16-17   Luke 5:17   John 12:27-30

When we refer to the "manifest presence" of the Holy Spirit, we mean He is showing Himself in the natural realm in some way. So, in the passage in Luke where the Spirit was present to heal, it means He was manifesting healing there. When Jesus was baptized, the Holy Spirit manifested as something like a dove. When Jesus prayed in front of the crowd, God manifested His voice in an audible way.

Sometimes you may feel His presence as you worship. You may feel tingling, or chills, or warmth, or pressure in some way. There's probably no end to ways He can manifest.

The Holy Spirit never leaves us or forsakes us because He's always in us. However, there are times He manifests Himself, He shows Himself in the natural realm. We can actually expect this, because Jesus taught us to pray, "Father, Your Kingdom come, Your will be done on earth as it is in Heaven."

When we pray that, we're calling heaven to earth. So, the manifestation of the Holy Spirit should be happening regularly as we do that.

MARCH 26

Why do we picture the Holy Spirit as a dove?

Read: Luke 3:21-22   Matthew 11:12

Have you ever noticed that God does not choose the things we would choose? For instance, Jesus is the Lamb of God. That's not a very powerful image on the surface. Jesus was born in a manger and not a castle, though He is a King. Jesus had no place to lay His head, though He owns the whole earth. Jesus had nothing about Him physically that would cause us to be attracted to Him, yet He draws all men to Himself.

Likewise, a dove is not known as a powerful bird. And yet, the Holy Spirit is the power of God! A dove is gentle and somewhat skittish, and while the Holy Spirit is gentle, He's also a force that cannot be overcome. The Kingdom of Heaven suffers violence and the violent take it by force. This cannot be done without the Holy Spirit.

We would expect the baptism of the Holy Spirit for Jesus to be more like what happened in the upper room in the book of Acts – a rushing wind and flames of fire. Instead, it looked gentle and peaceful, but was powerful and violent in the heavenly realm.

Prayer: Jesus, open our eyes today by Your Spirit to see in the Spirit, to see those things that are important and powerful, even when they seem small and insignificant and even powerless in the natural. We submit to You! Come, Holy Spirit!

MARCH 27

What does the down payment of the Holy Spirit mean?

Read: Ephesians 1:13-14   2 Corinthians 1:22
 2 Corinthians 5:5   Romans 8:23-24

Remember that the Lord said to be baptized into Christ includes water, Spirit, and fire; and the baptism isn't complete until it is all done, whether it happens all at once or separately.

John also testifies that the Father does not give the Holy Spirit by measure (John 3:34). So, if you have the Holy Spirit, you have Him! Therefore, we need not be confused by this.

The down payment of the Holy Spirit simply means that He is the guarantee of our future resurrection. We know that we are saved by the Holy Spirit living within us. (1 John 4:13 & 1 John 3:24) That salvation means that we will receive a resurrected body when Christ returns. Our hope is sure and will not disappoint.

The Holy Spirit in us is our guarantee of a future resurrection! Praise the LORD!

Does the Holy Spirit promote Himself?

Read: John 15:26   John 16:13-15

If the work of the Holy Spirit glorifies Jesus, then who would He be promoting? Obviously, He promotes Jesus. He does not promote Himself.

Some people who have seen the Holy Spirit in visions or with the eyes of their spirits, say that He is faceless. This is also how Kirk sees him – without a face! Whether or not He has a face or He chooses not to show it, the point is that He is not trying to bring glory to Himself. He lifts up Jesus everywhere He goes. He conforms us into the image of Christ. His power in us testifies of Jesus. His holiness in us testifies of Jesus. What He speaks testifies of Jesus.

Therefore, one way you can recognize if a spirit is from God or not, is whether or not it seeks glory for itself. While we do glorify the Holy Spirit, He is not seeking glory for Himself, but for Christ.

Prayer: Holy Spirit, we bless You! Praise You for testifying of and promoting the Lord Jesus Christ! Praise You Jesus! Praise You Father! Praise You Holy Spirit! Amen.

MARCH 29

The Holy Spirit speaks what He hears.

Read: John 16:13

The Scripture reading today should be familiar as we read this verse as part of yesterday's reading. But it is very important that we understand that what is brought to us by the Holy Spirit has come from Jesus, who has received everything from Father. Jesus is the Truth, and the Holy Spirit is called the Spirit of Truth because He tells us what He hears from the Truth.

As such, there is no lie in what He says, and there is not another way to arrive at the truth than besides the Holy Spirit. Without the Holy Spirit, we are guaranteed to be deceived. Remember that even when the demons cried out saying Jesus was the Christ, the Lord told them to be quiet. This is because we don't take anything from another spirit. We can only have the foundation of Christ through what comes by the Holy Spirit. Any other foundation will be shaky. This is why John writes in 1 John 2:21 that no lie is of the truth. If it has a little bit of lie and a lot of truth, throw out the whole thing! We want only truth from the Spirit of Truth.

Jesus was tempted by partial truths in Matthew 4, and the devil will try to tempt you with partial truths, too. Don't fall for it. It's the Holy Spirit who leads us into all truth, and not another spirit. Praise God for His Holy Spirit!

MARCH 30

Why does it seem like the Holy Spirit is so protected by God?

Read: Matthew 12:31-32

Why does it seem like the Holy Spirit is so protected by God? For instance, you can blaspheme Jesus, but not the Holy Spirit. Why? The Holy Spirit is God. If you reject Him, you reject God, remember? And yet, Jesus is God, and Father is God too.

Let's look at 1 Corinthians 2:11-12 (NKJV).

For what man knows the things of a man except the spirit of the man which is in him? Even so no one knows the things of God except the Spirit of God. Now we have received, not the spirit of the world, but the Spirit who is from God, that we might know the things that have been freely given to us by God.

So, without the Holy Spirit, we cannot know the things of God, right? Why would that be important? Look at what Jesus says in John 17:3 (NKJV).

"And this is eternal life, that they may know You, the only true God, and Jesus Christ whom You have sent."

Therefore, without the Holy Spirit, we cannot know God the Father, or Jesus. If we blaspheme the Holy Spirit, there's no more knowledge of God. He is the way Jesus has provided for us to know God. Therefore, that way is protected.

MARCH 31

When God does something, is it always through the Holy Spirit?

Read: Acts 1:4-8

Jesus had previously given what we call "the Great Commission" to His disciples in Matthew 28. But in Acts 1, He tells them not to leave Jerusalem until they had received the Holy Spirit, Whom He would send to them. So, He tells them to make disciples, but commands them to wait for the power to do so.

Do we think we can do any differently? Is there any way to do the works of God without the power of God? If the Holy Spirit is the power, and if our faith is to rest on the power of God, as Paul testifies in 1 Corinthians 2, then that is the way God operates. He does things through His Spirit.

Even the angels who do the Lord's bidding, do it by direction of the Spirit of God and with the faith God has given them. For example, the Winds of Change Angel blows the Wind of the Spirit to make change on the earth. It is the Spirit of God by which things are done and changes are made.

This is also why we cannot change on our own, but when the Spirit of Christ enters us, change happens.

What does it mean that the Holy Spirit is our Parakleet (Helper)?

Read: John 15:26   Romans 8:1-4   Romans 8:26

Without the Holy Spirit, we are doomed. We know that we cannot keep the written law. So, Jesus fulfilled the law for us. Now, we are to follow the law of the Spirit, which we also cannot do, except by the power of the Holy Spirit. He tells us what to do, and then He empowers us to do it.

It is absolutely true that all things are possible with God. And it's also true that nothing good is possible without God! The Helper is more than a natural help. He's the power of God living in us. Through Christ, we are partakers of the Divine Nature by His Spirit. He has given us His same Spirit to live in us to help us walk according to the Spirit and not the flesh. It is through the Holy Spirit we can do the things of God and live a holy, righteous life.

And as we read in Romans 8:26, He even prays for us when we don't know how to pray! What a Helper indeed!

Praise You Holy Spirit!

APRIL 2

Can you be holy without the Holy Spirit?

Read: 1 Peter 1:15-16   Hebrews 12:14   Galatians 3:3

The Lord commands us to be holy as He is holy. How is that even possible? Without being born again, it isn't.

Because of Jesus, we are able to have the Holy Spirit living within us. Without the Holy Spirit, we can't be holy. He's the One who makes us holy. As Peter testifies, we have become "partakers of the divine nature." That's incredible!

We are no longer made holy by trying to follow a bunch of written rules. No one could ever do it perfectly, anyway. Instead, Jesus fulfilled the law and the prophets for us, became sin for us, and then sent His Holy Spirit to live in us. He's totally cleansed us from sin and guilt and shame and then given us the same Spirit that lives in Him! We are holy as He is holy through His Spirit that lives in us!

Praise the Lord, Jesus Christ for what He has done and praise the Holy Spirit for making you holy, today!

APRIL 3

Can you be holy as He is holy?

Read: 1 Peter 1:15-16   Leviticus 11:44-45   Matthew 5:27-28, 33-37

The Lord commands us to be holy as He is holy. As we learned yesterday, the only way to be holy is by the Holy Spirit. But can we be as holy as He is?

When He first told the Israelites to be holy as He was holy, it was during the time of the Law. They could not do it. And now we know we are not under that law, but Jesus says we are under the Law of the Spirit, which as we read in Matthew, means we're under a higher standard than before!

Now we do not obey outward regulations that cannot change the heart. Instead, from a pure heart, we obey the Holy Spirit who leads us in paths of righteousness. We do this by the power of the Holy Spirit in the name of Jesus.

The Lord still tells us to be holy as He is holy, as Peter testifies, but now, we are able to do so through the Holy Spirit who lives in us. He is the One who makes men holy. Without Him, you are not holy. But with Him, you are holy as God is holy because the Holy Spirit is God.

Praise Jesus who gives us His Spirit to make us holy!

April 4

Following the Spirit will agree with Scripture.

Read: John 5:39   John 15:26 (NIV)

The Holy Spirit is called the Spirit of Truth because He is the Spirit of Christ, who is the Truth. And as John 15:26 states, the Holy Spirit will testify of Jesus. Therefore, what He brings to you, will be from Jesus. He's the Spirit of Truth who leads us into all truth.

Many times the Holy Spirit will speak to you from the Scriptures. While the Scriptures contain truth, remember that Jesus is the Truth and they testify of Him. Therefore, the Scriptures will line up with what the Spirit says because the Scriptures bear witness, or testify, of Jesus.

When you are listening to the Holy Spirit, which is hopefully all of the time, you can check what you hear by asking Him to show you in the Scriptures. So, say you hear something and you're not really sure it's God speaking, or it goes against something you've believed before, then ask the Holy Spirit to confirm it in the Scriptures. He will. And remember that the Holy Spirit is the one who interprets what the Scriptures mean, so be willing to give up what you think in order to hear Him.

Prayer: Holy Spirit, lead us into all truth! And when we need it, please confirm what you are saying in the Scriptures. Our faith will be built up! Praise You Jesus! Amen.

April 5

Will the Holy Spirit always avoid sharp words?

Wasn't Jesus filled with the Holy Spirit, and only spoke what He heard? What are some things He said?

Read: Matthew 23:13-15, 27-33

Looks like we have our answer. Jesus called the Pharisees, "whitewashed tombs," "sons of hell," brood(s) of vipers," "serpents," and more.

In the world, we're told to accept everyone, tolerate everything, and above all, "be nice!" But in the Kingdom of Heaven, not everything is tolerated. Not everyone is accepted, and not everything deserves a "nice" response.

"Be nice" isn't the gospel. Jesus is. He's the good news, and He's the Truth. Hebrews 4:12 says, **"For the word of God is living and powerful, and sharper than any two-edged sword, piercing even to the division of soul and spirit, and of joints and marrow, and is a discerner of the thoughts and intents of the heart."** (NKJV)

The Word, Jesus, pierces. He shines through to the darkest place and separates what needs to be separated. His Spirit is called, "The Spirit of Truth." As such, He cannot lie, and will not always avoid sharp words.

To those who are in Christ, we welcome this because we know that those who are sons are chastened by their Father. (Hebrews 12:5-8)

And a righteous man receives a slap in the face with gratitude (Psalm 141:5). It's those who oppose the LORD who don't welcome the sharp words, and it's really those who oppose the LORD to whom those words come from the Holy Spirit. The words to those in Christ may be correction from the Holy Spirit, but they are still always said in love.

GIFTS OF THE HOLY SPIRIT

APRIL 6

Expect, and by faith receive, gifts from the Holy Spirit, who loves you!

Read: 1 Corinthians 12:1, 7   1 Corinthians 14:1-4

For God so loved the world that He gave His only Son. Do you believe this? Do you understand that the Holy Spirit is the Spirit of Father and Jesus, Who love you? If you believe Father loves you and Jesus loves you, you must also believe that the Holy Spirit loves you, because they are One.

Furthermore, if you are in Christ, then your heart has been made good. Believing, then, that your heart is good and that the Holy Spirit loves you, go ahead and ask what you desire from the Holy Spirit.

He has good gifts and really desires to give them to you!

Command Satan to be removed from your presence and ask the Lord if there's anything He desires to say to you regarding these things.

APRIL 7

Gifts of the Holy Spirit – the Word of Knowledge.

Read: 1 Corinthians 12:4-8a, 11   John 1:48

As Jesus demonstrated with Nathanael, a word of knowledge is possessing information about someone that you couldn't possibly know, except by the power of the Holy Spirit. This is differentiated from knowing something about their future; that is a prophetic word. A word of knowledge is knowing something about someone from their past or current situation.

A word of knowledge may sometimes lead into a prophecy. For instance, I received the word "education" for a woman once. She admitted that she always wanted to teach. That led into prophesying over her God's destiny for her to teach.

The Word of Knowledge also manifests in your body sometimes. So, you may have a sudden pain in your leg and it's actually a word of knowledge that the person in front of you has an issue with their leg. You release that word of knowledge, and they are healed.

We have not because we ask not. Yet, the Lord is very generous and gracious. Ask the Holy Spirit to give you the gift of the word of knowledge. Then go out and practice it. Don't worry if you don't get it right. You'll get better and better as you step out in faith and practice this gift.

APRIL 8

Gifts of the Holy Spirit – the Word of Wisdom.

Read: 1 Corinthians 12:8   Mark 12:13-17

A word of wisdom is giving advice or instruction to someone regarding a situation, but not in a way that you could have come up with. So similar to a word of knowledge, it's really something you couldn't have known.

An example of this is when Jesus answered the Pharisees about paying taxes to Caesar. No one could have come up with the answer Jesus did, in this account. He basically sprung their trap back onto them.

When you operate in a word of wisdom, you will find yourself giving advice or instruction from the Holy Spirit. You will understand, even as you are speaking, that what is coming out of your mouth did not originate from you, but from God!

Ask the Holy Spirit to give you this gift and rejoice when you find yourself using it!

April 9

Gifts of the Holy Spirit – the Gift of Prophecy.

Read: 1 Corinthians 14:1, 3   Acts 11:28   Acts 19:6

Holding the office of a prophet is not necessary in order to prophesy. Anyone filled with the Holy Spirit can prophesy. Revelation 19:10 says that the testimony of Jesus is the Spirit of Prophecy. This is why it is the greatest gift. Those of us in Christ hold the testimony of Jesus and when we speak His words, we testify of Him.

Prophecy speaks forth what is to come, or how God desires it on earth. When you prophesy, you are seeing things the way God sees them. He calls forth the end from the beginning, and this is what you do when you prophesy. You're calling forth what is yet to come.

Today, ask for the gift of prophecy. Then in prayer, by faith, start prophesying over your loved ones, declaring what God has to say about them; in the name of Jesus!

April 10

Gifts of the Holy Spirit – the Gift of Faith.

Read: 1 Corinthians 12:9a

Everyone is given a measure of faith and the more you use it, the more you'll be given. However, the gift of faith is different from this. The gift of faith rises up in boldness beyond a normal faith. Apostles frequently have this gift, as do evangelists.

Someone alive at the writing of this devotional with this gift is Mike Evans. He leads the Jerusalem Prayer Team. One of his many stories is when the Holy Spirit sent him to New York and told him he had a room for him in the hotel that the Iranians had rented out. Mike went in there and told the clerk he had a room. The clerk told Mike that wasn't true. Mike insisted and kept saying he had a room until the guy gave him a key to a room. Then that weekend, he confronted the president of Iran at the time, Mahmoud Ahmadinejad. Mike pulled the page out of his Bible in the book of Daniel that says, "You've been weighed on the scales and found wanting," and gave it to Ahmadinejad. This was a bold move as the Iranian government was not known to be friendly to Jews or Christians, of which Mike is both.

Feel free to ask the Holy Spirit for the gift of faith, but then be ready to step out in boldness more than ever before!

APRIL 11

Gifts of the Holy Spirit – Gifts of Healings.

Read: 1 Corinthians 12:4&9   Matthew 12:9-14
         Acts 10:38

Gifts of healings is the ability to heal people, and it uses several of the gifts at the same time to do it. For example, someone may get a word of knowledge of some area of the body that needs healing, then they call out that healing and they know the person will be healed, which is the gift of faith. In this example, we see healing, faith, and word of knowledge all working together. That's the gifts of healings. Evangelists frequently have the gifts of healings.

Some people may have more specified gifts, like they have an anointing for backs or cancer, or headaches, etc. But the gifts of healings are bringing Jesus to people through healing, and most of the time, it's several of the gifts working together to get the job done.

Ask the Holy Spirit for the gifts of healings that you may bring Jesus to others through healing!

APRIL 12

Gifts of the Holy Spirit – Different kinds of tongues.

Read: Acts 2:1-4   Acts 10:44-46a
       1 Corinthians 12:10 1 Corinthians 14:4a
       Ephesians 6:18a   Romans 8:26 (NIV)

The Lord says tongues is one of the most powerful, yet unused, gifts that are available through the Holy Spirit. This is why the devil fights it so hard, trying to get people to think it's weird or ungodly.

Praying in tongues is surrendering yourself to the Holy Spirit. In this way of praying, the Holy Spirit prays through you because you don't even know what you're praying. You're completely surrendered to Him and trusting Him as He prays through you. It's the perfect prayer. It is humility to pray in tongues.

This is also a gift that edifies the person praying. This means when you pray in tongues, you are being made stronger. Hallelujah!

Ask the Holy Spirit for this gift and then open your mouth and pray, but not in a language you know! You will either pray in a known tongue – but not one you know. Or, you will pray in an angelic tongue – one that is not known on earth. Surrender, and allow the Holy Spirit to pray through you however He desires.

April 13

Gifts of the Holy Spirit – Interpretation of tongues.

Read: 1 Corinthians 12:10 1 Corinthians 14:4-5
1 Corinthians 2:9-12

When we pray in tongues, we receive edification. When tongues are interpreted, the church receives edification. Therefore, you can ask for interpretation that you may help others, for then this gift acts like prophecy.

The interpretation of tongues allows us to listen in on the heart of God. We are able to hear what the Holy Spirit is praying through someone. This is incredible because we hear the deep things of God.

Ask the Holy Spirit to give you interpretation of tongues, and then build up those around you by interpreting tongues when they are given.

Gifts of the Holy Spirit – Working of Miracles.

Read: Acts 2:22   Acts 8:6   Acts 19:11
          Matthew 20:30-34

All the gifts of the Spirit are miraculous, but there is a distinction between the all the gifts and then the working of miracles. Now, each believer should see miracles happen in their lives as they pray for people. However, a person that operates in the working of miracles will see miracles, distinct from healings, deliverances, words of knowledge, etc. Those are all miraculous because they are all from God, but the working of miracles, are like blind eyes opened, multiplying of food, lame people walking, or dead people being raised up. Someone with this gift sees miracles, not just healings, in their wake. Frequently, this gift operates with the gift of faith.

The Scriptures testify that Jesus operated in healing, deliverances, and miracles. The apostles and the evangelist Philip operated in miracles. You too can operate in miracles. Feel free to ask the Holy Spirit to give you the gift of the working of miracles. Call forth a creative miracle in someone you're laying hands on, as the Spirit leads you. Be bold.

The Holy Spirit wants you to ask for the working of miracles!

April 15

Gifts of the Holy Spirit – Discerning of spirits.

Read: 1 Corinthians 12:10   John 7:17   Luke 9:51-55
       Acts 16:16-18

The gift of discerning of spirits is given so that people can determine what manner of spirit a thing is from. It's not to be confused with discernment, which is not a gift of the Holy Spirit.

If you will to do His will, your heart is right to be able to discern what manner of spirit something is. We see this gift in operation when Paul casts the demon out of the little girl. The demon was saying what sounds right, but it was a wrong spirit. We see it again when the disciples wanted to call down fire on a town. Elijah did it, so why not? Well, they were operating in the wrong spirit at the time.

Those who operate in discerning of spirits will be able to discern where a spirit comes from (heaven or hell), and sometimes even the names of the spirits in operation.

Ask the Holy Spirit for the gift of discerning of spirits that you may know if something is of the Holy Spirit or an unclean spirit. And if a word is from an unclean spirit, discard the whole thing!

Pursuit of the Gifts of the Holy Spirit.

Read: Hebrews 11:6   1 Corinthians 12:31
       1 Corinthians 14:1

God is a rewarder of those who diligently seek Him. He desires to give more than we desire to get! He sent His Son while we were yet sinners. His desire to save us was even more than our desire to be saved, for we didn't even know we needed to be saved!

The Holy Spirit is One with the Father and the Son. There is no distinction. So, if the Father desires to give more than we desire to get, then the Holy Spirit also desires to give even more than we desire to get. Our pursuit of the gifts are more for us than for God. And it's much more rewarding to receive what you've longed for than to receive what you don't care about.

Therefore, desire the gifts of the Holy Spirit. He longs to pour out His gifts on you.

Can you have more than one gift?

Read: 1 Corinthians 14:1   Romans 8:32 (NIV)

Remember yesterday – the pursuit and desiring of the gifts of the Holy Spirit? The Holy Spirit gives as He wills, but He wills to give to those who want His gifts. Nowhere does it say you are limited to one gift. In your pursuit of the gifts of the Holy Spirit, don't limit yourself. Earnestly desire and pursue. God has said that along with Jesus, will He not *graciously* give us all things? He doesn't give begrudgingly, but willingly.

You can have more than one gift. So go ahead and talk to the Holy Spirit about this today. Ask Him which gifts He desires to give you and then ask for them. And don't become discouraged if it seems that you're not getting what you ask for. Keep pursuing. You won't be disappointed if you don't give up.

APRIL 18

If you don't have a particular gift, are you off the hook?

Read: Mark 16:15-18   James 5:14-18
       Luke 1:37

Just because you don't have a particular gift is no excuse to not do as Jesus is doing. His commission to us is quite clear, as laid out in Mark 16. He expects all of us to heal, deliver, raise the dead and save the lost. For example, even if you don't have the gift of healing, you can still lay hands on the sick and expect healing by faith, as James 5 indicates. With faith, all things are possible.

We've also been told by Jesus, as recorded in the Scriptures, that greater things will we do than Jesus has done. So, don't let the absence of a gift disqualify you from doing the greater things. Believe and go for it! All things are possible in Christ Jesus! Amen!

APRIL 19

Operating in the Gifts of the Spirit, as Jesus did.

Read: Acts 10:38   Matthew 14:14   Mark 5:19

How did Jesus operate in the gifts? As the Scriptures testify, He operated as a Man filled with the Holy Spirit in compassion and love. He left us an example that we should do as He has done. We are to operate in the gifts of the Holy Spirit by the power of the Holy Spirit in love and compassion as our Master showed us how to do.

Ask the Holy Spirit to give you His compassion for the lost, sick, broken, and hurting. Then remember to be aware of the Holy Spirit's leading as you go about your day. And be willing to have compassion on those around you as He leads you, using your gifts to bring about the Kingdom of Heaven in their lives.

APRIL 20

Jesus didn't do what He thought to do.

Read: Matthew 8:5-13 Matthew 8:14-15
John 9:1-7

Do you notice all the different ways Jesus healed and delivered? There are many more examples than the few we have read. He didn't follow a formula or what He thought might work. Jesus did what He heard and what He saw Father doing. He did not do what He reasoned in His intellect to do. We are to operate in the gifts of the Holy Spirit in the same way.

Be open to the different ways the Holy Spirit may tell you to minister. Be willing to use whatever gift He may show you, or to operate in your faith and authority.

April 21

Why would the Spirit give gifts to men?

Read: John 10:37-38   Matthew 14:14
        Matthew 15:32

Jesus did the miracles to prove God true. It's an evangelist's tool. The gifts of the Holy Spirit prove God is real and the Gospel is true, Jesus is the Son of God, and has really done what He said He did.

And as these gifts prove God true, they also prove God is love. Jesus was moved with compassion many times in the Scriptures, and each time proved to be powerful. He healed the sick, He fed the multitudes, He raised up those who were dead, etc. Compassion comes from love. It's different from sympathy in that it acts. When Jesus was moved with compassion, the gifts of the Holy Spirit were working through Him. He acted.

The gifts of the Holy Spirit working through Jesus, proved God true, even that God is Love, and the gifts of the Holy Spirit working through us will do the same.

Do you need to hold the office of evangelist to evangelize?

Read: John 4:28-29, 39   John 20:1-18   Luke 8:38-39

Was the Samaritan woman called an evangelist? What about Mary Magdelene? What about the man from whom legions of demons were cast out? The Bible doesn't record it as so, and Jesus never called them one. And yet, each of them evangelized. Each of them gave testimony of what God had done.

Though most of us do not hold the office of an evangelist, we can still evangelize. We can still do what evangelists do. They work on the front lines, bringing people into the Kingdom of God. They declare the gospel with power, and we can do that too. We can give testimony of what God has done and we can lay hands on the sick and heal, and we can cast out demons, and more.

We can evangelize even if we're not called by that title.

APRIL 23

Every disciple will evangelize.

Read: 2 Timothy 4:5   Matthew 28:18-20

Timothy was not an evangelist, and yet he was instructed to do the work of an evangelist. This is normal. Jesus said we were to go into all the world and make disciples of all the nations. This begins with evangelism.

If you are a disciple of Christ, you will evangelize. You really won't be able to help it. You live for Jesus and your desire is to see others live for Him, too. Therefore, don't worry if you're not called to the office of an evangelist. You can evangelize.

Prayer: Holy Spirit, we surrender to you. We choose to evangelize whenever you call upon us to do so. Empower us with your grace! In Jesus' name, Amen.

April 24

What is the message of Evangelism?

Read: 1 John 1:3 (NIV)

As John testifies, our desire is that others may have fellowship with us as we fellowship with the Father and with His Son, Jesus. So, our desire is to evangelize.

What is the message of evangelism?

All you really need to say to people is what you have seen and heard. That is your testimony of Jesus. What has He done for you? What have you seen Him do for others?

As you do this, you will also be walking in power because the gospel comes with power. The words you speak as you testify of Jesus will carry power. The acts you do, laying hands on people for healing, sharing a word of knowledge or prophecy, etc., will all come with power as you are led by the Spirit of the LORD.

The message of evangelism is Jesus. He is the Gospel and He comes with power. Expect it.

APRIL 25

Power Evangelism

Read: Matthew 9:2-8   Acts 28:7-10

Power forces a decision. Jesus evangelized in power, as do His disciples. Without power, it's an attempt to reach the intellect, which doesn't change the heart. And unless a person's heart is made new, they're not born again.

The Holy Spirit comes with power, and He works through us to evangelize. When we are listening and obeying, the words we speak are power. The acts we do are endued with power – because the gospel comes with it.

Remember that it's the mercy, or the kindness, of God that leads us to repentance. When someone is healed or delivered or given a word of knowledge or prophecy, they have encountered the kindness of God. They have encountered His power, and it cannot be taken from them. Now they can make a decision, not based on their intellect, but on the power of God. And it's the power of God that changes the heart.

APRIL 26

The Holy Spirit uses His gifts to evangelize.

Read: 1 Corinthians 12:4-11   Acts 5:14-16   Acts 8:39-40

The gifts of the Holy Spirit are given, not j for the edification of the church only, but also for the purpose of reaching the lost, among other things.

He desires to give His gifts to men. And while you may not have all the gifts, the Holy Spirit will make them available to you as you evangelize. When you are operating in faith, going out and doing what Jesus instructed us to do, you will start walking in power. The Lord cannot resist faith, and the Holy Spirit will enable you to do things you could not otherwise do as you step out and evangelize.

Do you think Philip, the Evangelist thought he could be caught up by the Spirit and brought to another place? (We call that being translated.) Well, the Holy Spirit is able and willing to give His gifts for the sake of evangelizing and He evidently didn't want to wait for Philip to walk there!

What about Peter's shadow healing people? Is there any substance to a shadow? Of course not, and yet the Holy Spirit enabled these miraculous healings. He desires us to evangelize and enables us to do so.

Therefore, even if you don't have a particular spiritual gift from the Holy Spirit, don't let that stop you from evangelizing. Expect the impossible to happen. Expect the gifts to flow anyway! God cannot be stopped! Halleluiah!

Do you think you have to be a Prophet?

Read: Hebrews 1:1-2 (NIV)   John 16:13-15 (NKJV)

First, command the atmosphere clear in the name of Jesus and then ponder these questions with the Holy Spirit:

How did God speak to His people before He sent His Son? How does He speak now that Jesus is in Heaven? How does it help your relationship with God if you don't have to hear Him through a prophet every time He talks? Can He still speak to you through other people, like prophets? Where does the Holy Spirit get the words that He says to us? Can you know things to come, even if you are not a prophet?

Secondly, ask the Lord to show you something to come. Wait on Him and allow Him to show you something, no matter how "big" or "small."

IN CHRIST

April 28

Can a good tree bring forth bad fruit?

Read: Luke 6:43-45 NKJV

If you are born again, is your heart good? According to the Scriptures, if your heart is good, can you bear bad fruit? Jesus says that if your heart is good, you can only produce good fruit.

But what about if you sin? What about if you don't follow correctly? Then what? What if you say something you shouldn't? Or, you don't say something you should? Then is your heart still good? Aren't you producing bad fruit?

Well, if you are in Christ, your desire is for righteousness. You can't help it. You are born again and have a new bent called "holiness." You actually desire what is good and right in your heart because Jesus has given you a new heart, and that's what He desires. You might make mistakes sometimes. You might even deliberately not follow the Holy Spirit sometimes. But, do you always repent?

The Lord says a repentant heart is a good heart. Even if you are deceived or miss the mark in some way, once the Holy Spirit brings it to your attention, you repent. Your heart is good, and therefore, produces good fruit.

Clear the atmosphere and ask the Holy Spirit about these things.

APRIL 29

What is the fruit of the Spirit?

Read: Galatians 5:22-25 NKJV

It's interesting to note that Paul writes if we are Christ's, then we have crucified the flesh with its passions and desires. Well, if we've done that, how can we <u>not</u> produce the fruit of the Spirit? This is not something we will have to try to do.

As you submit to the Holy Spirit, walking in Him, you will find yourself loving, being patient, having joy, being kind, etc. These are a byproduct of living in the Spirit. The fruit of the Spirit is something the Holy Spirit produces in us as we submit to Him, by walking in Him. This is Christ-likeness.

Today, thank the Holy Spirit for producing His fruit in your life. And choose to submit to Him and His ways.

APRIL 30

What about joy? Whose joy is your strength? Your joy, or God's joy?

Read: Nehemiah 8:10b

Compare your joy to His joy. Your joy is fleeting. It may depend on circumstances or feelings. If everything goes the way you desire, then you think you're having a good day. If things don't go as planned, the joy leaves and you turn grumpy.

Jesus' joy is eternal. It comes from the spring of life welling up in you. It does not depend on circumstances or feelings. It doesn't matter if things go as planned because you know that God works everything for the good of those who love Him. If it's not good, He's not done, yet. So, you have joy!

Look at Jesus. He went to the cross for the joy set before Him. He did all things for the pleasure, or joy, of the Father, even the cross. God always has joy, even in the midst of other "feelings." God truly does not have a bad day. If our eyes are on Him and we focus on His joy, couldn't the same be true for us?

What is the purpose of life?

Read: Ephesians 2:10 NKJV   John 17:3 NKJV
          1 John 5:20 NKJV

John 17:3 bears repeating here. **"And this is eternal life, that they may know You, the only true God, and Jesus Christ whom You have sent."**

To know God is not only eternal life, but the purpose of life. We are created to have a relationship with God and bring Him joy. He created us and then created a way for us to be with Him. Our purpose therefore, is to be with Him, to know Him, to be one with Him.

Life only has meaning in Christ, only has purpose in Christ; because without Christ, there is no knowledge of God.

Ponder these verses and thoughts with the Holy Spirit today.

MAY 2

A journey. Will you walk with Me?

Read: Amos 3:3 NKJV

Can two walk together unless they are agreed? It's an interesting question. There has to be agreement between you and God in order for you to walk together. So, then it begs the question: should God agree with you, or should you agree with God?

If there has to be agreement to walk together, one of you will have to give in to the other one in order to be in agreement. Why must you be in agreement with God in order to walk with Him?

Discuss these things with the Holy Spirit today and invite Him to walk with you.

Opinions.

Read: Ephesians 4:17

We're not supposed to walk in the futility, or uselessness, of our own thinking. Opinions are futile because they are our own thoughts. They are also a trap because once you give an opinion, you must then defend it. This defense of your opinion will come without the power of God. Therefore, you'll be striving to defend what you think.

As we saw yesterday, in order to walk with God, you need to agree with Him. His opinion is always the right one. This is why Jesus only spoke what He heard from Father. We can only agree with Him and with each other as we choose to agree with His opinion. Defending His opinion comes with His power because His words are powerful, in order that our faith may rest in the power of God and not the wisdom of men.

Ask the Holy Spirit to reveal areas of opinion to you and rejoice as He breaks them off of your thoughts!

MAY 4

What is the reward for bearing good fruit?

Read: John 15:1-2
___

If there's something in your life taking time and energy that doesn't bear good fruit, wouldn't you want it cut off? Conversely, what if there's an area that is bearing fruit? Wouldn't you want it to be even more fruitful? Yes!

Well, the way to bear more fruit is by pruning. That doesn't sound good on the surface, but it produces righteousness. Take faith as an example. The Lord gives you a measure of faith. Then He tests the faith. You pass the test, and He gives you more faith. The testing of your faith may not seem fun at the time, but when you look back, you realize how good it was for you to go through – how the testing strengthened you and produced more fruit.

Jesus is always looking for fruit, and the increase in fruit. Take the fig tree as an example. It wasn't the season for figs when Jesus cursed the tree for not bearing fruit. He expected fruit out of season! He expects fruit from us, too, so don't be upset at pruning. The Lord is working a work in you and will bring it to completion. Rejoice!

MAY 5

What does perfect peace look like?

Read: Isaiah 26:3 NKJV   John 14:27-28 NKJV

Jesus is our example of perfect peace. Yet, He got angry and threw merchants out of the temple. He also wept and was saddened at times. Somehow this may not look like Jesus was at peace all the time.

Is peace a feeling then, or something deeper and more permanent? If Jesus could be angry and throw merchants out of a temple and still be in peace, it means He was not out of control, nor out of faith. When we lose our peace, we tend to be in a time of doubting or unbelief. When Jesus says that He gives us peace and it's not as the world gives, it is not a peace based on circumstances or feelings. It is a peace that does violence in the heavenlies because we do not allow the enemy to set the agenda. We stay in faith, in peace, and trust in the Lord.

The Lord said that the Prince of Peace crushes Satan under His feet. That same peace is yours in Christ, today.

Speak to the Holy Spirit today about perfect peace. He wants to reveal these things to you.

There's one way. It's the Jesus way.

Read: Luke 13:24 NKJV   Hebrews 10:12

Jesus was answering a question in Luke 13:24. The question was — will only a few be saved? It's a good question. And why would there need to be striving, and why is it a narrow door?

There are many trying to enter another way — through works, through knowledge, following doctrines, adhering to a form of holiness, theologies, etc. Some are simply following a wolf in sheep's clothing.

Strive? Yes, to follow the Way, the Truth, and the Life isn't easy. And yet, the Holy Spirit empowers us to do that! We must cast off everything and follow! Jesus was the only one without sin, and so we can <u>only</u> enter through Him. *There is no other way.*

MAY 7

Strive to enter through the narrow gate.

Read: Matthew 7:13-14   Luke 13:24

We have learned that following the Holy Spirit is the Jesus Way. Hence the gate is narrow because there is only one way – the Jesus Way. Once you enter the narrow gate, the way remains narrow, for the path to following is narrow, as it is only one way. The path and the gate to destruction are wide, for it encompasses every other way.

Striving indicates that you are not entering by accident. It's intentional to follow the Lord. It's not easy because every other way is there, beckoning you to follow. And yet, with a heart turned toward the Lord and the power of the Holy Spirit in you, you can trust that He will keep you on the narrow path.

Ask the Holy Spirit to give you an undivided heart to follow Him down the narrow path, through the narrow gate, the one Way, who is Jesus, all the days of your life.

MAY 8

Look up! For your redemption is near!

Read: Luke 21:28   Romans 10:8

People look to many things to save them: money, work, people, government, etc. Our redemption is always found in Christ. No one and nothing in the world will satisfy, but Christ.

That redemption is always near, for He is found in you. He is the Living Word in your heart. Jesus holds everything together by the word of His power. Can we look to something else to fix our problems?

Call on Jesus today for your redemption, for He is very near!

Be still.

Read: Psalm 46:10   Mark 4:35-39

Peace, be still. Allow yourself to be still.

When the waves and wind quieted, it was because they knew who God was. You know God, too. The Holy Spirit desires you to be still today and listen to His voice. Allow the peace of Christ to still you. He is the LORD.

MAY 10

Come to Me all you who are weary and heavy laden.

Read: Matthew 11:28

Are you loaded down with the cares of the world? Are you weary or feeling worn out? Jesus is saying, "Bring it to Me! Bring Me your cares, bring Me what is wearing you out, bring Me weariness itself."

See yourself laying your burden on Jesus. He bore everything for you. Striving will get you nowhere fast. It only serves to create stress and weariness. Put it on Jesus. He really wants it.

Have you ever seen a sheep carrying a load for the shepherd? Sheep aren't meant to carry burdens. Allow the Shepherd to do it.

Prayer: Lord, I give You my burden. I come to You right now, Jesus, and give You all my weariness, all of my heavy load. Holy Spirit lead me as I give this up and choose now to follow.

MAY 11

I Am your sabbath rest.

Read: Hebrews 4:9-10 (Recommended reading: all of Hebrews Chapter 4.)   John 6:28-29

Jesus has become our Sabbath Rest. Under the Old Covenant, it was necessary for the people to take a day off a week and rest because everything they did was in their own strength. Under the New Covenant, we are born of the Spirit of Christ and everything we do is by the Spirit of the Lord, rather than in our own strength.

Therefore, a physical day is no longer our Sabbath Rest. Instead, we rest in the finished work of Christ, and by faith follow His Holy Spirit. Our work is to believe God just like Jesus said in John chapter 6. That believing is proven by our following. If we believe, we will obey. Hence, we will rest in Christ. It will not be striving, but the power of God working in us!

I want your burden.

Read: Luke 11:46 (NIV)   Matthew 11:28-30

Religion won't bear the burden for you. It loads you down with laws, principles, and rules you can't obey.

We can also become laden down with our own burden of sin. Jesus, remember, became sin for us. When the devil accuses, he does it with partial truths. Remember that he's a liar, so nothing he says is really true. But he'll take a partial truth and then mix it with lies, so that it's an out-and-out lie. If you do something wrong, the enemy will tell you that you did something wrong, and that you're bad. But are you really bad? Didn't Jesus take your sin and make you good? Can you see what's going on? It's all a lie from the enemy. Jesus wants to take that burden from you.

Jesus is the bearer of our burdens. He actually wants to take the load off of us. In giving Him our burdens, we take upon ourselves His yoke and His burden. In other words, we do the work the Lord is doing. That's why He says to take His yoke upon us and learn from Him. We learn to do it His way and it's no longer a burden for us. He has taken it from us!

Prayer: Jesus, take my burden! I give it to You and receive Your yoke and Your burden instead. I want to learn from You and do things Your way. Thank You for being willing to take my burden! Amen.

May 13

I became sin for you. I will never accuse you of sin.

Read: 2 Corinthians 5:17 & 21

Jesus didn't merely bear sin for you. He actually became sin for you, that you might become the righteousness of God in Christ. Talk about a **great exchange**!

So, if Jesus became sin for you, how could He ever accuse you of sin? Once you've been born again, that means you're now the righteousness of God in Christ. The old things are gone! You have been made new. Sin is done, left behind in the grave.

"The voice you hear that accuses is not Mine," says the Lord. "My voice is Love."

Command the enemy to be quiet and removed from your presence. Then ask Jesus to show you what it really means that He became sin for you. What you're really asking for is revelation into this topic. The Holy Spirit wants to reveal Jesus to you, so get ready to receive!

MAY 14

Without God, you're like a kid at a carnival/amusement park – looking for the next best rollercoaster or fun time.

Read: Ephesians 4:17-24

Each of us used to follow the dictates of sin before we were born again. We lived to please ourselves; much like going to an amusement park and getting on ride after ride after ride, only interested in having fun.

But what does the Scripture say? **"But you have not so learned Christ, if indeed you have heard Him and have been taught by Him, as the truth is in Jesus."** (v. 20-21)

This then is the difference. We have been taught by the Holy Spirit differently than we were taught by the world. The world teaches us to live for ourselves and do what seems best to us. The Holy Spirit teaches us to live for Jesus and do as He knows is best for us.

No longer do we live going from ride to ride, looking for a good time. Instead, we live day by day in the love of God and in the power of a resurrected life! That love conquers all fear and darkness. That power destroys the works of the devil. The fun for us has begun!

MAY 15

How do we know how to view ourselves?

Read: 2 Corinthians 5:17　　John 1:12
　　　　Colossians 2:9-10　　1 Corinthians 6:17

Psychology teaches us to look at ourselves to determine how we are. It teaches us the ways of fallen man to determine what's wrong with us. But looking within ourselves causes pride or depression. Both are selfish because they stem from looking at self.

We can't look within ourselves to see how we are. We must look to Him and see through His eyes. Jesus was tempted by the devil with the very thing that God said about Him. Father called Jesus His beloved Son. So that's what the enemy tried to get Jesus to doubt.

If you're in Christ, then you're also a child of God. If you're His child, how do you think He views you? Ask Him. How do you view your children, if you have them? Would you tolerate people saying bad things about your child? God doesn't like it, either. So don't say bad things about yourself. When you're in Christ, you no longer look at what you've done. You look at what He's done! And it's all good.

So today leave the grave behind you. That old man is dead. And ask the Holy Spirit how He sees you. Get ready to see with God's eyes!

What is holiness?

Read: Isaiah 6:1-3   Revelation 4:8
       Revelation 15:3-4

God alone is holy. Apart from Him, there is no holiness. Many people say that leaders of other religions are "holy men" or something to that effect. While that sounds like an honorable title to give someone, the only holy people on earth today are those with the Holy Spirit, for it is He who makes men holy.

Holy means to be sacred or set apart. It is completely pure and undefiled. But as we see in Revelation 15, God alone is the One who is holy. So "set apart" is not something people can do of themselves. It is only found in God. This is why when we're in Christ, He calls us "saints" or "holy ones." We've become partakers of Christ and been made holy by His Holy Spirit.

There is a great divide between holy and unholy and the only way to come from unholiness to holiness is through Jesus Christ. There is no other way to access the Holy Spirit who makes us holy than through the Son.

Holiness is God and God is holy.

How or why was Jesus holy?

Read: Hebrews 1:4   Luke 2:52   2 Corinthians 7:1

Was Jesus holy because He was God? Didn't Jesus come to earth as a man? Can God grow in stature and favor with Himself? Hebrews 1:4 says that Jesus obtained a better inheritance than the angels. Could God obtain an inheritance over that which He created?

It's easy to say that Jesus was holy because He was God. Or, Jesus did miracles because He was God. Or, Jesus could withstand temptations and suffering because He was God.

Yet, Hebrews 2:17-18 (NKJV) reads,

Therefore, in all things He had to be made like His brethren, that He might be a merciful and faithful High Priest in things pertaining to God, to make propitiation for the sins of the people. For in that He Himself has suffered, being tempted, He is able to aid those who are tempted.

Jesus came as a man filled with the Holy Spirit. In every way, He showed us what it looks like for us to live as a holy people. To be holy as God is holy, means we must have His Holy Spirit, which Jesus did. If we have the Holy Spirit, our bent is holiness. Our bent is no longer sin, but holiness. We desire those things that are of God.

Jesus taught us what it looks like to follow the Holy Spirit, perfectly. He perfected holiness and gave us the same Spirit that we may do the same as He did.

MAY 18

Why did Jesus call Himself the Son of Man?

Read: Genesis 1:27-28   Daniel 7:13-14   Matthew 9:6
        Matthew 16:13-17   Mark 14:61-62

In the beginning, God gave man dominion or authority, over the earth. Man gave that authority to the enemy when he sinned. So, it was going to take a man to get the dominion or authority, back from the enemy. Therefore, Jesus had to come as a man.

The Scriptures we read, and there are many more, testify that Jesus was called the "Son of Man." He actually became like those He created in order to redeem us. But it had to be known that He really was a man or else how could He save us? God cannot die, and Jesus had to die. God cannot be tempted, and yet Jesus had to be tempted in all ways like us. God cannot suffer, and yet Jesus had to suffer so we could be healed and delivered. God cannot become sin. Yet, the Scriptures say Jesus became sin for us.

As a man, Jesus also showed us what it looked like to be filled with the Holy Spirit and live by following the Spirit of God.

He became the Son of Man so that we could become sons of God.

Can we be considered sons?

Read: Galatians 4:1-7   Romans 8:14
       Romans 8:29-30

From the Scriptures we read, it should be obvious that we, not only *can* be considered sons, but that God ***desires*** us to be considered sons. He sent His Son into the world to bring many sons to glory (Hebrews 2:10).

And He also gave us the gift of the Holy Spirit to help us. For as Romans 8 testifies, it's those who are led by the Spirit of God who are sons of God. Remember that Jesus gave us an example as <u>the</u> Son of God, showing us what it looks like to live by the Spirit. Now, He's given us His same Spirit that we may walk as Jesus walked. The potential for sonship *is* there. By faith, believe you are a son, and allow the testing that proves it to come!

Command the enemy to leave your presence and command him to be quiet. Then ask Father about sonship. Ask Him about being a son. Tell Him you want to be a son and ask Him for revelation on it.

Would Jesus be considered our elder brother?

Read: John 3:16   Rom 8:29   Colossians 1:13-15
Hebrews 2:10-12

An older brother is someone you can look up to, someone that would be protective of his younger siblings, someone who would be expected to take over if the parents left, etc.

Jesus testifies of Himself that He is the only begotten Son of God. He is the One who came down from Heaven and it is through Him that we have access to God. Because of this, we can now be adopted as sons. This would make Jesus, our elder Brother, even though He is LORD.

As the Scriptures say, He is the firstborn among many brothers. He's the first and through Him, we can enter in, as well. Hebrews says that Jesus is not ashamed to call us "brother." He's not ashamed to acknowledge that we're part of His family. He's the One who made it possible!

Therefore, yes, you can consider Jesus, your Elder Brother. Praise God!

MAY 21

What does it mean to be conformed into the likeness of Christ?

Read: Romans 8:29   2 Corinthians 3:18

The Lord says, that as we behold Him, we are made like Him by the power of His Spirit. Does this mean we'll look like Him physically? Or, does it mean we'll act like Him?

People ought to know we are Christians by the way we live, not necessarily what we look like, right? So being conformed into the image of Christ, is being like Christ in all of our ways. This can only be done by the power of the Holy Spirit working in us. We can't make ourselves like Christ. But the Holy Spirit can. He breaks away strongholds until all we have left is Jesus.

This means He takes away poor thought patterns, habits, opinions, addictions, pride, basically anything that is not like Christ. And He replaces those things with the things that are of Christ – like love, faith, joy, humility, wisdom, etc.

Conformed into the likeness of Christ, is to be like Jesus. He's the One we want to be like and He's the One, Holy Spirit conforms us into.

Why is Jesus a Stone of stumbling?

Read: Matthew 21:42-44

As I thought about this devotional and Jesus being the stumbling stone, I smiled and was thinking of how amazing He is and how much I love Him – how sweet and precious He is. It seemed almost strange that I would be feeling love and joy when thinking of Him as a stumbling stone. But, then He brought me to 1 Peter 2:4-9 (NKJV).

Coming to Him as to a living stone, rejected indeed by men, but chosen by God and precious, you also, as living stones, are being built up a spiritual house, a holy priesthood, to offer up spiritual sacrifices acceptable to God through Jesus Christ. Therefore it is also contained in the Scripture,

*"Behold, I lay in Zion
A chief cornerstone, elect, precious,
And he who believes on Him will by no means be put to shame."*

Therefore, to you who believe, He is precious; but to those who are disobedient,

*"The stone which the builders rejected
Has become the chief cornerstone,"*
And
*"A stone of stumbling
And a rock of offense."*

They stumble, being disobedient to the word, to which they also were appointed. But you are a chosen generation, a royal priesthood, a holy nation, His own special people, that you may proclaim the praises of Him who called you out of darkness into His marvelous light...

Notice in these verses what He says about those who believe: we consider Jesus precious! But to those who are disobedient, the unbelieving, He is the Stone of stumbling. He is offensive. They stumble over Him because they will not accept Him as the Truth, Him as the Way, Him as the Life. Instead, they desire a different way, their own way, their own truth, their own life.

Yet, He sends out His word to all people. All people receive a witness, and to those who believe, it is precious. But to those who will not, they stumble, unless they come to the Light, being obedient to the word to which they were appointed.

Jesus became sin for us.

Read: 2 Corinthians 5:21

Jesus, the One who didn't even know sin – had never sinned – actually *became* sin for us. He didn't merely take the sin upon Himself, but He became sin. Why? That we might become the righteousness of God in Him. Not that we would *have* righteousness, but that we would *become* righteousness itself. Wow!

Therefore, if Jesus has become sin for us, is there any sin you have to bear? Do you have any sin left? What if you miss the mark and don't follow the Spirit in some area? Is that your sin to bear if you are in Christ? If Jesus became sin for us, then there's no sin left for us to take upon ourselves, right? He did it.

So, believe it and give it all over to Him. Start living as though you are the righteous of God in Him because if He became your sin, that's what you are!

Prayer: Praise You, Jesus! We accept fully that You became sin for us. Thank You. We accept also that because You became sin for us, we are now the righteousness of God in You! Amen!

MAY 24

What were we given at the death and resurrection of Jesus if we believe?

Read: 2 Peter 1:3-4 (NIV)   Ephesians 2:4-7, 14, 18-19 (NIV)
Romans 8:32 (NIV)

When Jesus became sin for you in death and rose again to life by the power of the Eternal Spirit of God, He made you the righteousness of God in Him. But that's not all!

Jesus made you a partaker of the Divine Nature, and every good thing that is in Him, is yours. God didn't spare His Son. Why would He hold back something lesser than Jesus? He won't.

Healing is yours. Deliverance is yours. Peace is yours. Wisdom is yours. Power is yours. Love is yours. Faith is yours. And yes, eternal life is yours in Christ.

Today, command the enemy away from you and ask the Holy Spirit to show you what Jesus has given you through His death and resurrection.

Blessing: May the God of our Lord Jesus Christ, the Father of glory, give you the Spirit of wisdom and revelation in the knowledge of Him. May the eyes of your understanding be enlightened, that you may know the hope of His calling, the riches of the glory of His inheritance in the saints, and what is the exceeding greatness of His power toward us who believe, according to the working of His mighty power which He worked in Christ when He raised Him from the dead and seated Him at His right hand in the heavenly places. Amen.

Further Reading: Isaiah 53:4-5

MAY 25

If you're in Christ, will your life be smooth sailing?

Read: John 17:14-15   Acts 9:15-16   2 Corinthians 11:24-27

There are many passages we could read for today's topic. In fact, read any of the gospels and see how Jesus was treated by the religious and you'll get an idea of what your life in Christ will look like.

Paul is a great example. He was told from the beginning of His born-again experience what he would have to suffer for Christ. And from what we read today, it was quite a bit, and that was only what he experienced to the point that he wrote his letter to the Corinthians. Some people believed Paul's message, but many did not, like they did for Jesus.

In like manner, some will receive you, but many will not. Those who will not, will oppose you. Yet, Jesus prays to the Father for us that while we won't be taken out of the world (out of our troubles), we will be kept from the evil one; meaning the evil one has nothing in us. You're promised peace, healing, salvation, wisdom, and much more, but you're also promised persecutions. As Jesus says in Mark 10:30, those who follow Him will receive much blessing, and with them persecutions.

Therefore, our life will not be smooth sailing in Christ, but remember – He walks on water and bids you to come! You're destined for greatness – the miraculous in Christ!

Further Reading: Mark 10:28-30

A vision, seeing through My eyes.

Read: Acts 9:10-16   Proverbs 15:3 (NKJV) 1 Samuel 16:7

In the reading out of Acts above, God gives instruction, warning, and insight that could not be known otherwise. He is no respecter of persons. So, what He does for the believers in Acts, He'll do for you. This is part of knowing Him.

In the other two passages for today's reading, we see that God's eyes are everywhere and He doesn't see only the physical, but He sees what is unseen. When He gives us a vision or a dream, He is showing us the unseen. He wants us to cultivate being able to see what is not seen. This is part of seeing through His eyes; because He sees it all.

Tell the Lord that you desire to see spiritually. Ask Him to open your spiritual vision to see through His eyes. Be persistent.

Command the enemy to be silent and removed from your presence as you do this.

MAY 27

An open vision – I want you to come with Me.

Read: Isaiah 6:1-13   2 Corinthians 12:1-8

In an open vision, you are taken somewhere to see what is going on in the heavenlies. Open visions are different from other visions. You are either really there in the body, or you are unsure if you are, because it is so real. These types of visions are not just for the prophets of old or the apostles in the scriptures. They are for each of us now. The Lord is desiring to show you what is happening and what is to come.

Believe what Jesus said about doing the "greater things!" Ask in faith for an open vision. Read John 3:34 (The Spirit is given without measure; you have the same Spirit that raised Christ from the dead!) Then read Romans 8:11.

Command the enemy away from you as you seek the Lord for an open vision.

If I can't get your attention, will you dream with Me?

Matthew 1:18-25 (NKJV)

Now the birth of Jesus Christ was as follows: After His mother Mary was betrothed to Joseph, before they came together, she was found with child of the Holy Spirit. Then Joseph her husband, being a just man, [the just shall live by faith, so he had faith] and not wanting to make her a public example, was minded to put her away secretly. But while he thought about these things, behold, an angel of the Lord appeared to him in a dream, saying,

"Joseph, son of David, do not be afraid to take to you Mary your wife, for that which is conceived in her is of the Holy Spirit. And she will bring forth a Son, and you shall call His name JESUS, for He will save His people from their sins."

So all was done that it might be fulfilled which was spoken by the Lord through the prophet, saying: *"Behold, the virgin shall be with child, and bear a Son, and they shall call His name Immanuel,"* which is translated, "God with us."

Then Joseph, being aroused from sleep, did as the angel of the Lord commanded him and took to him his wife, and did not know her till she had brought forth her firstborn Son. And he called His name JESUS.

Do you think Joseph would have made the right decision (to marry Mary) if he didn't have the dream?

Sometimes, we have so much going on that the Lord has to get our attention when we're unconscious! Think again about Joseph. There was a lot going on in his life. His fiancée was found to be pregnant, and he was concerned about what to do. So, in Joseph's case, God gave him a dream in order to get His word to him.

Today, ask the Holy Spirit to bring you dreams in the night. Invite the angels of the Lord to bring you the messages of the Lord as you sleep. Keep a journal by your bed and write down what you dream in the night. Then, after you dream, clear the atmosphere. Command the enemy to be quiet; and ask the Holy Spirit what your dreams mean.

Why is vision important?

Read: Proverbs 29:18a KJV   Galatians 6:9

We need to have a vision for the future. Without vision, we lose hope. Without vision, it's very difficult, if not impossible, to keep doing good. So often it looks like darkness prevails, and we end up "losing heart" without vision. In order to persevere, we need to know the end goal.

Perseverance is defined as (Merriam Webster): The quality that allows someone to continue trying to do something even when it is difficult.

How can you persevere without a vision – seeing the end? The Lord is very gracious to us and doesn't want us to lose hope. He will give us a vision for the future through speaking to us personally, through others, or through the prophets. He will not refuse to give you a vision of the future. He may not give it in all the detail you want, but He will give it.

Ask the Holy Spirit for a vision today and ask Jesus for the grace to persevere under any circumstance to see that vision fulfilled in your life.

Do you have a vision for your future?

Read: 1 Corinthians 12:12-27

In the above passage, we see that one part of the body has to help another. For instance, with our hands we wash our face, with our feet we move from place to place, with our ears we take in what someone is saying, etc. Yesterday, we talked about having a vision so that you could persevere. Did you hear from the Holy Spirit about that? Do you need help?

Ask for help, if needed. The body helps each other. Ask someone who hears God, who sees – perhaps a prophet or maybe someone who is prophetic. Ask them what the Lord shows them about you. Allow the Holy Spirit to lead you to the person He desires to help you.

You will reach the goal through love.

Read: 1 Corinthians 13:1-3 NIV

Goals can be reached many ways. Look at history. Men have reached their goals to dominate through wars, famine, oppression, and brute force. Athletes have reached their goals to win medals through rigorous training, hours of sweating, and strict diets. People reach the goal of retiring and taking life easy in their last years on earth by working many hours and saving money.

The Lord has given you a vision for your future. That is your goal. But, you won't reach it through any worldly effort. You will only attain your vision, your goal, through love. Jesus doesn't give you a goal that you can attain any other way. His way is love, and every other way is worthless.

Choose love.

WISDOM & REVELATION

JUNE 1

Those who have ears, let them hear.

Read: John 3:6 (NKJV)   Matthew 13:10-17 (NKJV)

Those who are born of the Spirit have ears to hear, meaning they hear the mysteries of God and understand them. They are not dull, but perceptive into the things of God. Your spirit has ears and when you are born again, your spirit is hearing and understanding.

The mysteries of the Kingdom of Heaven are not understandable to the natural man because they come from the Holy Spirit. They are the deep things of God that are only understood by the Spirit of God. Without the Spirit of God, there is no understanding.

Therefore, the mysteries of God are given to you to understand when you have ears to hear.

Command the enemy to be quiet and ask the Holy Spirit about these things.

June 2

Those who have eyes, let them see.

Read: John 3:3 (NKJV)

Yesterday, the Lord spoke to you about having ears to hear. Now, He is speaking to you about having eyes to see. Why wouldn't you be able to see the Kingdom of God without being born again?

The answer lies in the Holy Spirit. Without new eyes of the Spirit of God, you cannot see. You are blind. The Holy Spirit awakens your senses. Where you were dead, you are now alive. Where you couldn't see and hear, now you can. Those who are not born-again of the Spirit of God do not understand these things. But once you are born of God's Spirit, you see and you hear.

Command the atmosphere clear, around you. This will help you hear the voice of the Lord and see clearly. Then ask the Holy Spirit to speak to you regarding this. Also, ask Him to show you the Kingdom of God. Write down what you see and hear.

JUNE 3

Today is your day to receive wisdom.

Read: 1 Corinthians 1:30a NKJV   1 Corinthians 2:4-16 NKJV

If Jesus became wisdom from God for us, is there anywhere else we should look for wisdom? He is wisdom. And we receive this wisdom through His Spirit who dwells in us. This is the same Spirit who tells us the mysteries of God. These mysteries are wisdom.

To be in Christ, means His Spirit is in you. He wants you to operate in wisdom. He wants you to have faith that if you ask for wisdom, He'll give it to you. (See James 1:5.) And He's telling you that He will give you wisdom, this very day!

Surrender your thoughts and receive wisdom (Christ) today. Today is your day to receive wisdom.

June 4

What is wisdom?

Read: Colossians 2:2-3   1 Corinthians 1:18-25 NKJV

We learned yesterday that Jesus became wisdom for us. Today, we see that all knowledge is hidden in Christ. And wisdom is commonly said to be the proper use of knowledge. If this is true, and you know that all knowledge is hidden in Christ, where will you go then to get wisdom?

You know the answer is Jesus. He is where we look to get wisdom, then. By His Spirit, we may know the deep things of God. And it should be obvious from today's reading in 1 Corinthians how God views any "wisdom" that is not from Him. If wisdom outside of Christ is foolishness, why would we even bother with it?

Talk to the Holy Spirit today about what wisdom is.

JUNE 5

The Holy Spirit leads us into all Truth.

Read: John 16:13-15

In our theology, our study of God, we must have an understanding that it is the Holy Spirit who leads us into all truth. There's not another way to arrive at the truth, other than through the Holy Spirit. He is the Spirit of Truth. Therefore, if we want to know truth, we will need to be listening to the Holy Spirit and believing what He says.

Any other way people may think they can arrive at the Truth – other than the Holy Spirit – will not work. This includes much study, college degrees, debating, and any way other than listening to and submitting to the Holy Spirit. Jesus said that the Holy Spirit would take of what belongs to Him and declare it to us and that all that the Father has are His. That means nothing is left out. If we want truth, we'll find it in Jesus, who is the Truth. And Jesus sent the Holy Spirit to us to lead us into that truth.

Prayer: Come Holy Spirit! Lead us into truth. We submit to You!

June 6

The teachings of men.

Read: Colossians 2:8   Matthew 15:9   2 Timothy 4:3
1 Timothy 6:3-5   2 Timothy 3:5

Yesterday, we learned that only the Holy Spirit leads us into all truth and any other attempt to arrive at the truth will fail. One of those "other" ways is the teachings of men.

Our brains, or our intellects, are really just a good option to following the Holy Spirit. So sometimes people will teach things contrary to the truth because they have decided they've figured out the right way. Others will deliberately teach demonic doctrines. Either way, if it's not from the Holy Spirit, it's a lie. It might even have partial truth in it, but if it's not from God, discard the whole thing.

And as you decide what to believe as truth and what to discard as a lie, make sure you are asking the Holy Spirit. The gospel comes with power, so there will be witness from the Holy Spirit when it is truth. The words will carry power and the messengers bringing the truth will walk in power. Don't fall for what looks good or sounds good without first checking with the Holy Spirit. He wants to tell you the truth. So, trust that He will.

Prayer: I break off all false doctrines of men in your life now, in Jesus' name. Holy Spirit, we invite you to lead us into all truth!

JUNE 7

The origin of your theology.

Read: Galatians 1:6-12

Paul testifies to the Galatian church, the gospel we believe must come by revelation from Jesus Christ. If it does not come from Jesus, it's coming from the demonic realm. James testifies in chapter 3 of his book, that there are two kinds of wisdom. One is earthly and demonic, and the other is spiritual. Those of us who walk by the Spirit, are those who receive the spiritual wisdom. That wisdom is heavenly. Those who walk by the flesh are those who receive the earthly, demonic wisdom. That wisdom is from hell.

The origin of our theology matters. Where does something come from? We can only follow the Spirit of Truth and not the spirit of falsehood. Jesus says in John 7:17-18, **"If anyone chooses to do God's will, he will find out whether My teaching comes from God or whether I speak on my own. He who speaks on his own does so to gain honor for himself, but he who works for the honor of the one who sent him is a man of truth; there is nothing false about him." (NIV)**

Therefore, turn your heart to will to do the Lord's will, and you will understand if the theology you believe is from God or not. Theologies that do not come from God will frequently come through people seeking their own glory and not the glory of the One who sent them.

Prayer: Holy Spirit, please reveal anything we believe that is not truth. Break its power in us. We yearn to do your will. If there's a stronghold, we're believing that's a lie, we are asking you to expose it and give us grace to believe truth. Amen.

JUNE 8

The doctrine of demons.

Read: 1 Timothy 4:1-2   John 8:42-47

We've touched on this topic in the previous days' devotionals, but today the Lord wants to really expose the doctrine of demons.

Knowing the origin of our theology like we learned yesterday will expose the doctrine of demons. The enemy is the father of lies, so every lie originates from hell. Therefore, anything being brought to you to believe that has even a little bit of a lie in it, is not from God. Remember that the Holy Spirit leads you into all truth. He doesn't lead you into a little truth and a little lie, and then you have to figure it out. He leads you into *all* truth.

The demonic is trying to lead you into lies and they'll do it a little at a time, if necessary. But look at an airplane. If it flies even a degree off the trajectory of where it needs to go, it won't take long for it to be completely off course. That's what will happen to us, if we let in little lies here and there.

That being said, do not live in fear of the doctrine of demons, but continually fellowship with the Holy Spirit. Bring Him what you are hearing, reading, and seeing, asking Him to confirm if it's truth or if it's from hell. (He may confirm truth through a person or the Scriptures, among other ways.)

Prayer: Lord, we praise you for the truth. We want Jesus and nothing else. Holy Spirit, lead us and keep us away from the doctrine of demons. In the name of Jesus, Amen.

You say you believe the Bible, why don't you believe it?

Read: John 5:37-40   Matthew 22:29

Jesus testifies that a person can search the Scriptures and not really believe them. They can know what things say, but not the meaning behind it. Saying you believe the Bible is meaningless without faith accompanying it.

In other words, you need to mix your reading of Scripture with faith. The Bereans searched the Scriptures eagerly after listening to the Apostles speak. They were filled with faith and looked into the Scriptures with faith. The Lord says these were of more noble character than others because of it. (Acts 17:10-12)

There are many things written in Scripture that can offend us when the Holy Spirit reveals their meaning to us. Jesus is saying He doesn't want us offended or in disbelief because those Scriptures testify of Him, and they don't bear false witness.

Today, command the enemy to leave and be silent. Then ask the Holy Spirit to speak to you about believing what is written in the Bible. Write down what He says.

JUNE 10

Apologetics? (Can you argue someone into Heaven?)

Read: 1 Corinthians 1:18 – 2:7   Philippians 3:3-11

Paul testifies that Christ Jesus became for us wisdom from God. Therefore, if we want wisdom, it will only be found in Christ. Paul was a very smart man. He was very educated, and he knew how to argue. As he, himself, said, he was a Pharisee of Pharisees. So not only did he obey the law, but he knew all the rules and the Scriptures. But did that save him? Did any of that knowledge save him?

Of course not. He needed to be knocked off his donkey and struck blind so that he could finally see. From that point on, he walked in the power of God, healing the sick, raising the dead, shaking off snakes in the fire, and speaking words of life.

There's no argument when it comes to Jesus. It's "game over." The power of God cannot be argued. Therefore, instead of arguing with someone about faith in God, try operating in the wisdom of Christ and the power of the Holy Spirit, that the disciples you make will base their faith on the power of God, instead of the wisdom of men.

JUNE 11

The Tree of Life.

Read: John 15:1

The Holy Spirit gave Kirk a vision in which he saw a really big tree with lots of fruit on it. There were people climbing the tree and eating the fruit and having a blast! There were other people on the ground who were watching, and they were thinking those eating the fruit were foolish. Some walked away and thought it was crazy.

Regarding this, the Lord says that the Tree of Life is hard to come to and easy to walk away from because it requires humility. It requires one to be dead to self, every day. It's always putting the Holy Spirit, first.

But if you choose the Tree of Life, you won't regret eating the fruit, even if others think you're foolish!

Talk to the Holy Spirit about what this means. Think beyond just getting saved.

JUNE 12

The Tree of the Knowledge of Good & Evil.

Read: 1 Corinthians 1:18-25
___

The Lord says that the Tree of the Knowledge of Good and Evil sucks you in like a vacuum cleaner. Once you receive what's on that tree, you can't do without it. And once you eat of it, you think you know. And you can't understand why people won't listen to you because, after all, you know and they need to know what you know.

Knowledge puffs up, but love builds up. (1 Corinthians 8:1) Love is humble, not proud. The Tree of the Knowledge of Good and Evil causes people to be proud. It resists humility and blinds the eater to its true nature.

Resist the urge to eat from the Tree of the Knowledge of Good and Evil. Instead, submit to the Holy Spirit each day, deciding you don't really know anything unless God reveals it to you.

The Two Trees & the Old and New Wine.

Read: Luke 5:37-39

The word "better" at the end of verse 39, actually means "easy" or "manageable." So, Jesus is saying that the old wine is more manageable.

This is why the new wine is rejected. It is because of the nature of the trees. The Tree of the Knowledge of Good and Evil is knowledge, therefore, it is manageable. You can manage it, like the old wine. It's easier.

The Holy Spirit manages the Tree of Life. It's the same with the new wine. The Holy Spirit is that new wine and you can't manage Him. He does as He pleases, just as the wind blows where it wills. (John 3)

God allows the knowledge from the Tree of the Knowledge of Good and Evil to be titillating. That word means "pleasantly stimulating, or exciting." It draws people in because it makes them feel in control. They can manage it. However, like old wine, the Tree of the Knowledge of Good and Evil is actually intoxicating.

Resist the urge to "need to know." Knowledge is an impediment to following the Holy Spirit. Choose instead to live by faith, trusting the Holy Spirit to lead you in all things, not your knowledge.

The Tree of the Knowledge of Good & Evil makes you like Satan.

Read: Genesis 3:4-5 James 3:16

The devil said eating from the Tree of the Knowledge of Good and Evil would make Adam and Eve like God, but it didn't. It's the same lie he uses today. When we eat of it, it doesn't make us like God. It makes us like the devil.

The Tree of the Knowledge of Good and Evil makes you see what you don't have. Satan saw something he didn't have and wanted it. It's what caused him to fall, and it's what causes man to fall.

The Tree of Life, on the other hand, makes you like God because God says, "Eat of this tree and I'll give you everything."

Romans 8:32 says, **"He who did not spare His own Son, but gave Him up for us all – how will He not also, along with Him, graciously give us all things?"** (NIV)

One tree makes you hungry. It never satisfies. The other makes you full. It always satisfies.

JUNE 15

When we read the Bible, is there any priority to what we read? For instance, should we read more of what Paul wrote, or of what Jesus said?

Read: 1 Corinthians 11:1 (NIV)   Romans 8:29-30
       John 6:63

As the Scripture says, we are being conformed into the image of Christ, not someone else's image. Jesus also said that His words are Spirit and they are Life. So those are the words we want to focus on.

And yet, Paul tells the Corinthians they should follow Him as he follows Christ. That means that in the same manner in which Paul follows Jesus, he wants those who are under his authority to follow Jesus, too.

The likeness of Christ is the goal. We're not being conformed into the likeness of Paul or of someone else, but the likeness of Christ Jesus, Himself. Therefore, all Scripture is profitable and useful for teaching, but the words of Jesus should primarily be our focus because it's Him we're after. He's the Mediator of the New Covenant.

Therefore, if we read something Paul or someone else wrote and our understanding of it doesn't line up with what Jesus said or Jesus did, then we need to question our understanding of what that person wrote. We always must bring everything back to Jesus. He's our Lord. He's our focus. He's the One we listen to by His Spirit.

Prayer: Holy Spirit, please give us revelation of Jesus, as we read the Scriptures. Praise You!

JUNE 16

Why does it seem like Paul wrote things that were contrary to each other in the Scriptures?

Read: Hebrews 5:12-6:3

The writer of Hebrews gives us great insight into the writing of apostles. Taking the Apostle Paul as an example, he frequently wrote rules for his churches, and those rules seemed to contradict each other at times.

For example, in one case he would tell a church he didn't permit a woman to preach. In another case, he would say there's no difference between men and women and that a woman apostle, named Junia was highly esteemed among the apostles.

Looking at what we read in Hebrews, today, gives us a great picture of immature believers as opposed to mature ones. Immature believers will sometimes need rules to help them as they learn to follow the Holy Spirit, and apostles have the authority to make rules according to the believers' needs. Mature believers will not need many, if any, rules as they follow because they've learned to follow well.

For example, in 1 Timothy 2, Paul tells Timothy, he doesn't permit a woman to preach. Well, it needs to be understood that the new church in Ephesus struggled with women who were used to dominating because the idol of their city was female. These women then came into the church and expected to do the same there. They expected to lead simply because they were women, and not necessarily because they were called into a leadership position. They needed a rule to help them as they learned to follow the Spirit of Christ.

Another example is when the apostles in Jerusalem told some of the Gentile believers that it seemed good to them and to the Holy Spirit to give them a few rules to help them. These rules, however, were not for the entire church of Christ. And as apostles make rules, the rules change as those who learn to follow change.

It's very similar to raising children. We give our children rules when they are young, but then as they mature, we get rid of rules they don't need and maybe impose new ones until they are mature and don't need anymore rules. This is what an apostle does. The goal is Christ-likeness, or maturity. Therefore, as believers mature, rules made by their apostles will become less and less, if they are needed at all.

JUNE 17

Besides what Paul wrote, there are other things written in Scripture that seem to oppose each other. Why?

Read: Proverbs 26:4-5

These two proverbs are a great example of contradictions in Scripture. One proverb instructs us not to answer a fool according to his folly or we'll be like him. The very next proverb tells us to answer a fool according to his folly or else he'll think he's wise. Which is it?

The answer is: it's both! There are times you will answer a fool according to his folly and there are other times you will not. But how do you know when to do one and when to do the other? You listen.

The answer to the things that seem contradictory in Scripture is listening and following. What would the Holy Spirit have you answer this time? One time, He may tell you to speak. Another time He may tell you to be silent.

Jesus sometimes answered those who accused Him of evil, like when He called the Pharisees sons of the devil. Other times He kept quiet as He was accused, like He did in the presence of Pilate.

How did He know what to do at different times? It goes back to Matthew 4:4 – **"Man shall not live on bread alone, but by every word that proceeds** [currently comes forth] **from the mouth of God."** Therefore, our answer is in hearing God and doing what He says.

JUNE 18

What does 1 Corinthians 1:20 mean?

Where is the wise? Where is the scribe? Where is the disputer of this age? Has not God made foolish the wisdom of this world?

Read: 1 Corinthians 1:18-25

Men love to argue and debate, but the Holy Spirit doesn't debate. That may surprise you because many men claim to be arguing and debating on behalf of God. They come up with all sorts of theologies and what they believe to be iron-clad cases that are water-tight against any argument. But have you ever noticed no one ever really wins a religious debate? It's useless.

However, when someone shows up with the power of God, it puts an end to all argument. In one healing, God makes foolish the wisdom of men. In one word, God can shut the mouths of his enemies against Him.

Remember when the religious leaders tried to trap Jesus regarding paying taxes to Caesar? Jesus told them to give Him a coin, asked them whose picture and inscription were on it, and then told them to give to Caesar what was his. End of discussion. There is no argument. There is no debate. There is power.

Remember, the time the religious leaders tried to trap Jesus into breaking the Sabbath laws by bringing into the temple a man with a withered hand. Jesus healed the man and asked the religious leaders if it was lawful to do good or do evil, to save a life or destroy it?

They had no answer to the power of God. The Holy Spirit comes with power and ends debate and argument. While it's true that those with a religious spirit may still want to oppose you after you come with power, they cannot refute it.

Jesus always wins! And God makes foolish those who think they know something when they know nothing. Amen!

JUNE 19

What does it mean to be "woke," and can a follower of Christ be "woke"?

Read: James 4:4

Followers of the "woke" culture believe they are awake to racial discrimination, prejudices, and social injustices, where other people are unaware of what they see as "reality." In this "woke" reality, everything revolves around injustice because of the color of one's skin or some perceived prejudice against their choice of gender, etc.

These woke followers then raise their voices and put pressure on others to conform to their way of thinking and take action against those they perceive to be racist or discriminatory in some way. Doesn't sound too terrible, does it?

Read Revelation 2:18-29.

To be woke as a believer, means to allow the world to dictate what is right and what is wrong. In this account, in Revelation, Jesus is addressing a church that allowed someone with an evil spirit to dictate right and wrong. She was seducing people with her teachings. They actually thought they were right, and they were wrong.

The world cannot do right. This is why Jesus exited the desert with a message of repentance and preached the Kingdom of Heaven. The Kingdom of God is completely contrary to the kingdom of the world. They are at odds with each other. You cannot be a friend of

God and a friend of the world. You cannot serve two masters, because the Scriptures say you will hate one and love the other.

Woke-ism is wrong for a believer. Allow the Holy Spirit to tell you right and wrong. He's the One who leads you into all truth. And don't be seduced by the power of nice sounding lies. You have one cause. His name is Jesus.

Prayer: In the name and authority of Jesus, and in the power of His Holy Spirit, I break off the lies of woke-ism from each of us. And, Holy Spirit, we invite you to bring us truth. Amen.

Can a pastor really be woke?

We've heard of pastors who are "woke." Is that a possibility for a pastor, really? Or any of the five-fold ministers?

Read: Matthew 6:19-21, 24

Most of the time, we look at the passage we just read in regards to money or things we own. However, anything you elevate higher than Jesus is an idol, not only money or objects. This means desiring others to think well of you could be an idol. Looking good to the world could be an idol. Looking like you're nice could be an idol.

The woke mentality elevates a way of thinking above God. Those who are chosen by Christ should have nothing above Him.

For a pastor who is truly chosen by Christ, one who follows Jesus, it is not possible that they would be "woke." Jesus says His five-fold ministers have died to self and those who are dead to self, live only for Him. That means they don't have an agenda somewhere else. If they do, they haven't really died to self.

It's possible for some in the five-fold to be deceived sometimes, but that is also why there are apostles and prophets. They correct the others in the five-fold when necessary and are themselves corrected by each other when necessary.

If you see a pastor who is woke, he is either not chosen by Christ, or he is deceived. Jesus is not "woke" and neither are His ministers.

What about ideologies? How do we know what's right to believe?

Read: Ephesians 4:17-24

Ideology is defined as ideas or beliefs that are shared by people of the same group. Ideologies could be called doctrines, as well.

As Christians, we understand that the truth is in Jesus. In fact, there is no way to arrive at a knowledge of the truth other than through the Holy Spirit because He is the Spirit of Truth who leads us into all truth (Jesus being the Truth).

Therefore, all of our ideologies, or our beliefs will be in Christ. What did Jesus say? What did Jesus do? He is the exact representation of Father (Hebrews 1:3). So, if we want to know what God is like, we must look at Jesus. He is perfect theology.

We know what is right by listening to His Spirit and His apostles and prophets who are the foundation, laying the Cornerstone, who is Christ. To them is given revelation for the church. The prophets hear and the apostles reveal the meaning of what is heard. That is Christ.

And in all of this, the Holy Spirit in you will bear witness of the Truth because Jesus said the Holy Spirit testifies of Jesus.

Prayer: Holy Spirit testify of Jesus to us. When we hear the truth, You will bear witness and by Your grace, we'll recognize that witness. Bless us with greater sensitivity to You in all things. Thank You! Amen.

JUNE 22

Can a good thing become a stronghold?

Read: Psalm 27:1   Nahum 1:7   1 Samuel 24:22
           2 Corinthians 10:4

There are various references to strongholds in the Scriptures. A stronghold was somewhere people went that was fortified and strong so that the enemy could not reach them. David escaped Saul by going to a stronghold, and we find refuge in Jesus, Who is our stronghold.

But in 2 Corinthians 10:4, we read that we're to use spiritual weapons to take down strongholds that exalt themselves against Christ as Lord in our lives. These are any thoughts that come against Jesus, as Lord. We generally think of these things as bad things, but can good things become a stronghold, too?

Read: Mark 7:1-9

Traditions frequently start as something good, but can often get in the way of following the Holy Spirit. Even words that God has spoken to us in the past we can exalt so high that we cannot follow the fresh word that comes from the Holy Spirit. Therefore, when we say that Jesus is our Stronghold, that means we follow every freshly spoken word He speaks. He is alive, not dead. So, He continually speaks. And if we're not willing to change with what He says, we'll end up building a stronghold out of something that was good and exalting it above Christ.

Jesus has to be the stronghold.

Prayer: In the name of Jesus, I ask You, Holy Spirit, to expose and break any stronghold in my life that has exalted itself above Jesus Christ. He alone is My LORD and no other. I open myself to You. Have Your way, Lord Jesus! Amen.

JUNE 23

How do we decide if something like a "word" is from God or not?

Read: John 7:15-18

In this passage of John, Jesus is showing what it is like to be an Apostle. Apostles may never study or go to seminary, but they bring the doctrine that is not theirs, but Father's. They do not speak on their own authority, for they seek the glory of the One who sent them.

This then is also how we know if a word is from God or not. Is the person speaking seeking their own glory? Are they lifting up themselves, or the Lord? Does the word come with power and authority? Does the Holy Spirit bear witness?

For those of us who desire to do the Lord's will, these questions will be quite easy to answer because we do not have a separate agenda. We have a firm foundation because we listen to His voice and obey what He says (think of the house built on the rock). We actually yearn to do His will. Therefore, when we hear the voice of the Holy Spirit through others, we will recognize His voice – even if we don't necessarily "like" what we've heard. For, we've died to self and truly live for Christ.

So then, knowing if something is a word from God or not is easier than you might think. But don't let your intellect, or your logic, talk you out of it. Remember that faith doesn't need to understand. It believes and allows understanding to come later.

LAW OF THE SPIRIT

Do you believe that Jesus fulfilled the Law and the Prophets?

Read: Matthew 5:17   John 17:4   Hebrews 6:18

Jesus said, He came to fulfill the law and the Prophets. He also said He finished the work Father gave Him to do. The writer of Hebrews testifies that it's impossible for God to lie. So, Jesus wasn't lying when He spoke these things.

Jesus said He finished the work Father gave Him to do, and fulfilling the law and the Prophets was part of that work. Is there any law or Prophets you have to fulfill? Do you still have to obey a law in order to be blessed? Or, is there something the prophets commanded in the Old Covenant that's still applicable to you under the New Covenant?

Command the enemy to be silent and speak to the Holy Spirit about this.

JUNE 25

If the Law has been fulfilled, which part of the Law do you obey?

Read: Galatians 5:1-4

If you choose to obey even a part of the law, you are indebted to obey the whole thing. This is because if you put yourself under part of the law, you've actually put yourself under the whole lLaw. No one, except Jesus, has ever been able to obey the whole law.

If you could obey the law, why would Jesus need to come? In that case, you could attain righteousness on your own.

Therefore, the Spirit says to you today, put away the law. It is not a part of you. Look to the law of the Spirit by listening and obeying. The Spirit of Truth will lead you into all truth.

Do you get extra credit for obeying the Law?

Read: Romans 3:21-22, 28

If we're justified by faith, apart from observing the law, then what benefit would it possibly give you to obey the law? And how could you? There are 10 commandments in stone and over 600 other laws. Jesus said He fulfilled *all* the law and the Prophets. It's an affront to Jesus to think you need to obey the law when He took care of it for you.

The Lord says your "grade" cannot improve. There's no improving on what Jesus has done. We simply cannot improve on the Lord. Therefore, there is no extra credit for obeying the law. You have been set free!

Praise the LORD!

What is the Law of the Spirit?

Read: Romans 7:6   Galatians 5:18   Hebrews 8:7-13

We do not live under a written code, but by every word that comes from Father. This is how Jesus defeated the enemy in the desert. Each time He was tempted, He answered by what He heard Father saying to Him.

Now, all things from Father have been given to Jesus, who gives them to us. Jesus has actually sent us His Spirit – the Holy Spirit – so that we can follow Him. The Holy Spirit brings us what Jesus says and empowers us to obey what we hear. The Holy Spirit leads us into all truth and leads us in paths of righteousness.

This, then, is the Law of the Spirit. It is the words of Christ brought to us by His Spirit who dwells in us.

Today, listen for the voice of the Holy Spirit in all that you are doing. And obey when you hear.

JUNE 28

There is no condemnation for those in Christ Jesus.

Read: Romans 8:1   John 3:17

Condemnation came through the law because it made manifest our sinfulness without any help to rectify it. The Spirit, however, brings life. He does not bring condemnation for those in Christ Jesus.

As you listen to the Holy Spirit, as thoughts go through your mind each day, learn to recognize which thoughts are condemnation and reject those. The Holy Spirit will convict you, but not condemn you.

Prayer: Jesus, thank You that You have set us free from all condemnation. Holy Spirit, lead us into all truth today.

JUNE 29

The Holy Spirit invites you into a relationship.

Read: John 14:15-18

The Holy Spirit invites you into a relationship. The law invites you into theology, because the law deals with your intellect, and the Spirit deals with your heart. The Lord is after our hearts.

Today, command your intellect to be subject to your Spirit, to your heart, and invite the Holy Spirit to take you deeper into a relationship with Him.

JUNE 30

Have you learned how to love?

Read: 1 John 4:7-12, 16 (NIV)

The Lord wants to show us what it means to live by the law of the Spirit. The greatest command under the Old Covenant according to Jesus is to love – to love God and love your neighbor as yourself. Is there anything greater than love? Not according to 1 Corinthians 13:13 where it says, "the greatest of these is love." So, even under the New Covenant, love is the greatest command. Whatever we do in following Jesus, must be done in love.

Yet, until we are born again, we really can't love because God is love and if we're not in God, we really don't love. Often, we need to learn to love. Love is patient. Love is kind. It does not envy. It does not boast. It is not proud. It is not rude. It is not self-seeking. It is not easily angered. It keeps no record of wrongs. It does not delight in evil, but rejoices with the truth. It always protects, always trusts, always hopes, always perseveres. Love ***never*** fails. (1 Corinthians 13)

Can you say this about yourself? Are you still learning to love? Sometimes God has to point out something to us, because we don't even realize we're not loving. Other times we know better, but our old man tries to climb out of the grave and cause us to live in the old way, and not the new way of the Spirit.

God is Love. Therefore, to live in God means to live in lLove. So, by faith, choose love. Ask the Holy Spirit to give you the grace to love as He loves, to even *be* love as He is love. The greatest rewards of heaven go to those who love.

JULY 1

Can you be patient today?

Read: Romans 8:1-5   Galatians 5:22-23 (NIV)

Jesus told us in John 14:15 that if we love Him, we will obey what He commands. Well, how can we know what He commands without listening to the Holy Spirit?

Today, He is asking us if we can be patient. Isn't patience a fruit of the Spirit? Don't we who follow Him have the Holy Spirit? Don't we follow the law of the Spirit, which would include patience? If He says patience is a fruit of the Spirit, then isn't the grace (or empowerment) there to be patient?

So, can you be patient, today? You absolutely can! When Jesus tells us to do something, the grace comes with the command. For the Word of God comes with the power to perform itself. In other words, you have the empowerment by the Spirit of the Lord to do what He tells you to do. Of yourself, you can do nothing, but in Christ, all things are possible.

This, too, is how Jesus is glorified, for people know that our lives are lived supernaturally when we follow the Holy Spirit. The things that would make other people impatient will not make us so. The things that make others angry, mean, unloving, and unforgiving, do not do the same for us. For we walk by the Spirit in love, kindness, patience, and forgiveness.

Again, can you be patient today? Yes, you can.

JULY 2

If you can see that I (the Lord) have been kind, could you also show kindness to those I love today?

Read: John 13:14-17

Is Jesus only talking about washing feet, in the passage we just read? If He is our Lord and Master, wouldn't we be doing what He is doing all the time? Therefore, if He is showing kindness to those He loves today, as He says, wouldn't we be doing the same?

A disciple does as his master does. In this case, we are the disciples and Jesus is our Master. We do as we see Him do. This is why the 72 healed the sick, cast out demons, and preached the Kingdom. Their Master did it. This is why Peter walked on water. His Master was doing it.

So, can you show kindness today? How can you not? If Jesus is showing kindness and He is your Master, then you too can show kindness. Remember yesterday we learned that His words come with power. If He tells us to do something, the power is there to do it.

Therefore, in love, show kindness today to those the Lord is showing kindness to. Ask the Holy Spirit who He is showing kindness to today? Then go and do likewise.

JULY 3

Do you have jealousy in your heart?

Read: James 3:14-16 (ESV)

"But if you have bitter jealousy and selfish ambition in your hearts, do not boast and be false to the truth. This is not the wisdom that comes down from above, but is earthly, unspiritual, demonic. For where jealousy and selfish ambition exist, there will be disorder and every vile practice."

Some translations use the word "envy" instead of jealousy. The words are similar. In a basic sense, it means you don't like it that someone has something you want.

The Lord is telling us to check our hearts because jealousy opens the door to "every vile practice" or every evil thing. It's actually demonic because it's rooted in self-seeking, which opposes love.

The love of self is rooted in all sin, which is why we must die and be born again. Self needs to go. Search your heart with the Holy Spirit, asking Him to reveal any jealousy today and then repent of it, if you find any in your heart.

Where there has been any jealousy, start blessing the person you were jealous of. Start asking the Lord to give them what you desire for yourself. You'll see the jealousy lose all power and love take its place.

Prayer: Lord Jesus, forgive me for jealousy. (Name the person or area.) I repent. Deliver me from it and give me Your eyes, Your thoughts toward this situation instead. Praise You, Jesus, for deliverance! Amen.

JULY 4

Bragging doesn't come from Me.

Read: Jeremiah 9:23-24 (NIV)   James 4:16 (NKJV)
       1 Corinthians 4:7 (NIV)   Luke 14:7-11 (NKJV)

If you were confident in your standing with God, would you need to brag or boast to anyone about yourself, your accomplishments, your calling, your family, your anything? If you allow the Lord to lift you up, He will exalt you at the right time.

Resist the urge to boast and brag. Instead, allow the Lord to lift you up at the right time because bragging doesn't come from Him. And if it doesn't come from Him, then it's coming from the enemy. We can't let the enemy set the agenda.

Today, ask the Holy Spirit to convict you when the thought comes to lift yourself up. Then thank Him for stopping you from bragging.

JULY 5

Can you see that arrogance keeps your eyes on yourself?

Read: Psalm 75:4-7   1 Timothy 3:6 NIV   James 1:17

We are still discussing the law of the Spirit. Can you tell how it is different from the written laws yet?

Yesterday, we talked about how bragging does not come from God. Bragging is arrogant. If we are arrogant, we are thinking too highly of ourselves. Isn't this what the devil did? Didn't he look at himself and decide that he was really something and that he ought to be God?

If we are arrogant, we are looking at self, not at God. Remember the Scripture from yesterday that said whatever good we are, or whatever good we have, didn't originate with us? Every good and perfect gift comes down, not from within ourselves; it comes down from the Father who loves us.

When we look at ourselves, there are two things that can happen. One is that we'll be puffed up in pride. The other is that we'll feel ashamed and condemned. Either way, though, it is arrogance. Arrogance looks at self – period. Even depression is self-centered, for it is the enemy's way of making us look at us. It doesn't matter if you come away thinking you're better than you are, or worse than you are. It's all arrogance. It's all eyes on self.

Keeping our eyes on Jesus will totally thwart the enemy's plan for us to look at ourselves.

Prayer: In the name of Jesus, I break off all lies of arrogance. I command the enemy away and declare his lies are exposed. Jesus, I want to look at you and not myself! Help me! I choose humility and not arrogance. Holy Spirit, I believe You empower me to look at Jesus. Thank You! Amen!

The Old Testament explains the Old Covenant.

Read: Exodus 20:1-21

Have you ever noticed that the Old Testament reads differently than the New Testament? This is because the Old Testament of the Scriptures was written for those who were under the law. The Old Testament, especially the first five books, goes to great lengths to explain the Old Covenant. The covenant that God made with His people at the first was one where they needed to obey in order to be blessed. If they didn't obey, they were under a curse. It was completely based on man's ability to obey. And because man couldn't do it, more and more rules were added to "help" him. (The 10 commandments were not the only rules.)

People were required to listen to God, but they listened through the prophets. Additionally, no direct access to God was offered. Instead, people had to access God through a priest. These priests were chosen by God according to their lineage and had to adhere to strict rules in order to be considered holy.

When we read the Old Testament, we must keep in mind that it's written to those under the law, and it's written in such a way as to lead people to follow according to the law because it explains the Old Covenant. Therefore, if we do not read it with the Holy Spirit, we will tend to make laws, rules, and principles out of it. Then we will try to follow the laws, rules, and principles we've made, instead of the Holy Spirit.

All Scripture points to Jesus, so read the Scriptures that way, not as though you're under the Old Covenant.

Additional reading: Deuteronomy 30

The New Testament explains the New Covenant.

Read: 2 Corinthians 3:6, 15-18   Hebrews 8:7-13

Jesus became the Mediator of the New Covenant. In this Covenant, the Holy Spirit indwells the people who are thus expected to hear His voice and are also empowered by Him to do acts of service. This covenant is no longer based on man's ability to follow laws, but it is based on what Jesus did in man's stead.

Hebrews 9:14 (NKJV) reads, **"... how much more shall the blood of Christ, who through the eternal Spirit offered Himself without spot to God, cleanse your conscience from dead works to serve the living God."**

Now, you are not only cleansed for a year on the outside, but your inside is clean forever! You no longer have a guilty conscience. You are no longer bound to sin! The New Testament explains this.

As a New Covenant believer, our Lord and Savior, Jesus Christ, is not only our example and our model, but we are also being made into His image. We are therefore expected to follow as He followed. He (Jesus) said that He could do nothing on His own, but only did what He saw the Father doing. He did not follow the "letter" (the law), but only the Spirit. And because He followed the Holy Spirit, everything He did lined up with Scripture.

This is what the New Testament explains to us. It shows us how to follow the Holy Spirit, showing us what Jesus accomplished and how that accomplishment looks in a born-again believer's life. It's really all about Jesus and following His Spirit; for how can we be like Him unless we have His Spirit and follow Him?

Jesus is the Teacher of the New Covenant.

Read: Hebrews 9:11-15 (the blood of bulls and goats cleansed the outside, but Jesus cleanses the inside)
Matthew 7:28-29   Luke 24:13-27

Who would be better qualified to teach the New Covenant, than the One who is the Mediator of the New Covenant? If we want to live in the New Covenant, we look at Jesus.

The things written in Scripture that Jesus taught and said explain the New Covenant to us. The apostles, who have revelation from Jesus, teach us because Jesus is the Teacher of the Covenant He made on our behalf. This is why Paul could say in Galatians that he didn't receive his revelation from any man, but from Jesus Himself. This is because Jesus is the Teacher of the New Covenant.

Therefore, the understanding we receive about the New Covenant should be coming from the One who mediated it, our Teacher, Jesus.

Why is it said that the New Covenant is a Covenant of Jesus' blood?

Read: Hebrews 9:16-28

The Old Covenant was put into effect, or became effective, by the sprinkling of blood of bulls and goats on the people and objects it was used to make holy. In a similar fashion, the New Covenant is put into effect by the pure blood of Jesus, Himself.

The Old Covenant was done away with as soon as Jesus gave His blood. The shedding of His blood meant there was a New Covenant, or New Agreement, with God. The old agreement holds no power anymore, for the new agreement supersedes it.

Therefore, the reason we can say the New Covenant is a Covenant of Jesus' blood is because without the blood of Jesus, there wouldn't be a New Covenant. We would still be required to obey laws we couldn't obey and shed the blood of animals on a regular basis, whose blood could never take away our guilt. Now the blood of Jesus cleanses us from all sin (1 John 1:7). And we overcome the enemy by the blood of the Lamb (Jesus) and by the word of our testimony, loving not even our lives anymore as they have been exchanged for His Life, through His shed blood. (Revelation 12:11)

Thank Him for the New Covenant that is written in His blood and not written in words on a page.

Additional Reading: Hebrews 10:1-25

Explanation of the "Mercy Seat" and the blood.

Read: Exodus 25:18-22 (Moses meets with God, Who is above the mercy seat.)
Leviticus 16:2, 14-17 (High Priest requirements.)
Hebrews 9:1-15, 12:24, 4:16 (Jesus puts His blood on the Mercy Seat in Heaven.)

There is a lot of Scripture reading today because some explanation of the Mercy Seat is required. The things Moses made for the Tabernacle in Israel were copies of what is in Heaven. Therefore, under the Old Covenant, there was a Mercy Seat above the Ark of the Covenant in the Holy of Holies. This Mercy Seat would be sprinkled with blood once a year by the High Priest. It is said that they would tie a rope around the High Priest's ankle so that if he died in the Holy of Holies, they could pull him out. No one would want to go and retrieve him, because no one was allowed into the Holy of Holies except the High Priest. And he only went once a year, and never without blood. Unallowed access meant sure death.

Under the New Covenant, Jesus took His perfect, sinless blood and sprinkled it on the Mercy Seat in Heaven, of which the earthly one was only a copy. Because of this, we are able to access the Holy One who sits enthroned over the heavenly Mercy Seat. Jesus has made a way through His body, through His blood – the blood that cries out "mercy" on our behalf! He has made us holy and we can enter boldly into the Holy of Holies in Heaven itself and meet with our Father, God.

Praise the LORD Jesus Christ!

JULY 11

What's the difference between living under the Law and living under Grace?

Read: Leviticus 13:42-46   Mark 1:40-43
       Hebrews 10:14-22

The difference between living under the law and living under grace is the difference between life and death.

The example of leprosy is one example of what it looks like to live under the law or under the grace. In the Old Covenant, a leper had to be expelled from the camp. Lepers were not allowed to come near other people. Under the New Covenant, the leper is healed and set free. One is death and the other is Life.

Under the law, no one could enter the presence of God, except the High Priest and he could only go once a year with blood. Under grace, we may enter God's presence all the time with boldness!

Under Law, people had to obey written rules exactly or be punished. Under grace, the Holy Spirit puts His laws in our hearts and our minds, empowering us to obey what He says, and God no longer even remembers our sins!

Truly the difference between law and grace is life and death. But as Paul writes, **"[T]he law of the Spirit of life in Christ Jesus has made me free from the law of sin and death."** (Romans 8:2)

July 12

How was death's power removed by Jesus?

Read: Hosea 13:14 NIV   1 Corinthians 15:54-57

Isaiah prophesied about Jesus: **He will swallow up death forever, And the Lord GOD will wipe away tears from all faces; The rebuke of His people He will take away from all the earth; For the LORD has spoken.** (25:8 NKJV)

We see in 1 Corinthians 15, that Jesus destroyed death forever. The sting of death is sin. Yet, Jesus became sin for us; therefore, sin is off the table for those in Christ. It's not a consideration.

And Paul goes on to say that the strength of sin is the law. Yet, didn't Jesus fulfill *all* the law and the prophets for us? Then the law is done away with, too.

Therefore, Jesus removed the power of death by getting rid of sin and getting rid of the law. In the New Covenant these are not things that have power over us. Yes, there's still sin in the world, but the power is in you to walk in righteousness. And yes, there are still those who follow law and rules and principles, but the power is in you to follow the laws written on your hearts and on your minds – the law of the Spirit as the Scriptures says.

The power of death is removed by Jesus, and when we live in Him, following the Way, the Truth, and the Life, death no longer has any power over us whatsoever! We are free!

Praise Jesus today for removing the power of death over you!

JULY 13

Are there any of the Old Covenant Laws that must be followed by the New Covenant believer?

Read: John 14:15   Matthew 5:17-20

Jesus says, if we love Him, we will keep His commandments. Does He mean the 10 commandments given to Moses for Israel? How can that be if He fulfilled all the law and the prophets?

Read Galatians 3:1-14.

Seems contradictory, doesn't it? Paul is showing us what Jesus really meant when He said those who love Him obey His commandments and that our righteousness has to exceed that of the Pharisees. For, who obeyed the law better than the Pharisees? We certainly couldn't do better than them, but in Christ, all is fulfilled. So the only way to exceed their righteousness is by becoming the righteousness of God in Christ.

This is what Paul means by walking in faith as opposed to following the law. The two are in opposition to each other. You are either in faith or under law. You can't have both because the law is not of faith.

Therefore, put away all the laws you've been told to follow. Instead, follow the Spirit, Whom you received by faith. The commandments of Jesus will be told to you by His Spirit. He's the One who leads you into all truth. You're not under law, but under grace.

Further reading: Galatians 3:19-25

JULY 14

What does it mean to have the Law in our minds and in our hearts?

Read: Hebrews 10:15-16   Romans 8:2-6

The writer of Hebrews quotes the prophet Jeremiah regarding the law being written on our hearts and on our minds. The Lord was prophesying through Jeremiah that the law the people were familiar with following would be done away with, in order that they might follow Him by His Spirit instead. This law in our minds and our hearts, is a living law. It is not something written in stone, that brings death. It comes from the Spirit of Life and brings life.

Now, we who are in Christ have died to ourselves in order that we might live for Christ. To live for Christ, we must follow His Spirit. Following His Spirit requires listening and obeying. The Holy Spirit speaks to our hearts and tells us what we must do. Our minds are also in subjection to Him. That is why we must take every thought captive and bring it into obedience to Christ – because only those thoughts coming from the Holy Spirit are the ones we should be entertaining.

"Written in our minds and in our hearts" is the work of the Holy Spirit. Hence, Paul can write, **"The word is near you, in your mouth and in your heart."** (Romans 10:8) Jesus is that Word and the Holy Spirit brings Him to us in our hearts and in our minds.

Therefore, if you are following the Holy Spirit, you will not go wrong.

JULY 15

You only "win" by the Spirit, not by the intellect.

Read: Zechariah 4:6

We only win if we do things by the Spirit of the LORD. Because if we do something by the flesh, it is we who receive the glory and not God.

The intellect of some is very mighty, very powerful. But one word from the Spirit of the LORD and those mighty, powerful intellectual thoughts are shot down.

Those who argue by the intellect will come with laws, theologies, rules and principles that are not provable, except by the intellect, which will twist what the Spirit of Christ is truly doing or saying. A religious spirit has no power, except what it derives from a legalistic viewpoint. Therefore, the law is the power of sin. But the Lord has made us faithful ministers, not of the letter, which brings death, but of the Spirit of Christ, who brings life!

Therefore, do not lower yourselves to legalistic details. Instead, simply speak *life* according to the Spirit of Life! God does not lose, and you cannot win, except by His Spirit! Amen.

PRAYER

JULY 16

How do you know what to pray?

Read: 1 Corinthians 2:10 & 12   Ephesians 5:17

How do we know what to pray? Do we pray what we think or what seems good to us? Doesn't the Scriptures say that there's a way that seems right to a man, but its end is death? Then praying whatever seems right to us is not the way to go.

The Lord desires us to know His will, and we know that will through His Spirit. This knowledge includes our prayers. Doesn't God know what you should pray? If He says you should know His will, then ask Him how to pray. Don't assume you know. Ask, and pray by faith what you hear.

What if you don't know what to pray?

Read: Romans 8:26 (NIV)

Praying in the Spirit, or praying in tongues, is the perfect way to pray. When you pray in tongues, the Holy Spirit is praying through you. He can never be wrong because He's the Spirit of truth! So, whenever you don't know what to pray, or you think you're not hearing how to pray, then use your prayer language (tongues).

The more you do this, the more you will start to understand His will in situations you didn't understand before. You'll also start receiving wisdom in areas you didn't before. And sometimes, when you ask how to pray, the Holy Spirit will prompt you to pray in tongues. Go for it! Don't ever be afraid to pray in tongues. God partners with us to get His will accomplished on earth, and part of that is our prayers. So, we definitely want to be praying into His will. Tongues are a great way to do that.

Do not pray in agreement with your adversary.

Read: Luke 9:51-56

In this passage, the disciples wanted to call down fire from Heaven because people rejected Jesus. Calling down fire from Heaven was something Elijah did twice to captains and their fifty men, and once he called down fire on the altar to prove God was God and Baal was not. So, the disciples had scriptural backing to their desire.

The problem was that their reasoning behind calling down the fire was not from Heaven. To do so in this case would have been to agree with the enemy and not with God. We must know what spirit we are praying from. Is it from the Holy Spirit, or is it from Hell?

Ask yourself these questions: Do you think you know what other people need? Do you think you know what others should be doing? Or what God should be doing?

The enemy will work with our pride that we "know" how something should be. Instead, we need to align our hearts with God's, and ask Him how to pray so that we are in agreement with Him and not the enemy.

Therefore, when you pray, command the enemy to be silent and then ask God how to pray.

JULY 19

The enemy disguises himself as an angel of light.

Read: 2 Corinthians 11:14

All authority has been given to us through Jesus Christ. (Matthew 28:18) This means the enemy has no authority, except what we give him. Therefore, he's going to try to deceive us into giving him authority, so that he can carry out his wicked schemes.

The enemy will make it look good to you to pray his way. What he brings to you will usually tickle your intellect and sound "right." It may even come with some scriptural backing. But, remember that the disciples had scriptural backing, too, when they wanted to call down fire from Heaven to burn up a city and everyone in it.

Don't give the devil your authority by agreeing with him. The enemy's authority comes when you agree with his lies.

Command the atmosphere clear around you. Then speak to the Holy Spirit about these things, asking how to pray regarding whatever He has placed on your heart.

JULY 20

Anger, bitterness, and offense allows Satan to set the agenda.

Read: James 3:14-16 (NIV)

These verses in James are really to the point. If you have envy and selfish ambition, you will find disorder and ***every*** evil practice. That doesn't leave anything out, as far as darkness goes. Allowing these evil things opens the door to all the other evil things, like anger, bitterness, and offense. When we open the door to the demonic by agreeing with their lies – lies of offense, lies of envy, lies of selfishness, lies of bitterness, etc., we empower the liar. Then he's the one who sets the agenda.

We cannot allow this. It all starts with where our eyes are focused. Are our eyes focused on self or on God? If they are focused on self, we become self-seeking, envious, bitter, angry, offended, etc. When they are focused on God, we are thankful, loving, kind, peaceable, gentle, humble, etc. When our eyes on ourselves, we pray in agreement with the devil. When our eyes are on God, we pray in agreement with God. He, then, is the One who sets the agenda.

Ask the Holy Spirit to reveal anywhere you've been allowing the enemy to set the agenda. Turn from it and ask the Lord how to pray in agreement with Him.

What is God's agenda?

Read: John 10:10   Psalm 37:4

Jesus is the exact representation of Father. If you want to know what God is like, you simply need to look at Jesus. What did He do and what did He say?

Jesus said that He came that we may have life, and have it more abundantly. That's God's agenda: abundant life. As His ambassadors, we bring that abundant life to earth. It's called the Kingdom of Heaven, and it's within us. Or rather, He's within us!

That brings us to the Scripture reading from Psalms. When we delight ourselves in the Lord, He gives us the desires of our hearts. If you are delighted in the LORD, would your eyes be on yourself? Of course not. Your eyes would be on Jesus, and you would know the desires of your good heart are good!

Put your delight in the LORD, in what He is saying and doing, and agree with Him. Then you will know His agenda.

Is prayer asking for things or talking with God? (back and forth)

Read: John 10:27

When you talk with someone, are you the only one who does the talking or, is there some back and forth? Maybe you say something and then the person you speak with replies, etc? Hopefully, when you speak with someone, you allow them to speak, too. That's how you truly get to know someone. You talk back and forth with them. You interact with them.

When we pray, therefore, we should not only talk **to** God, but we should talk **with** God. We should not just come to Him with a list of things we are requesting, say amen, and walk away; thinking we've prayed. He says in Scripture that He already knows the things we need before we even come.

He wants to talk with us. What He has to say is way more important than what we have to say. However, He does want to hear us. He does want us to talk, but He wants us to listen, as well.

Jesus said His sheep know His voice. You recognize someone's voice that you hear often. You can be in a room filled with people and if you hear your mom speak, you know it's her. It's the same with the Lord. You know His voice, but it takes time in His presence, listening, talking back and forth.

Allow yourself to talk back and forth with the Holy Spirit, today. Keep a record of what He says to you as you do this.

JULY 23

Ask Me how to pray.

Read: Matthew 6:33   Ephesians 5:15-17

When we seek the Lord first, His Kingdom first, His righteousness first (meaning the right way), it means we're hearing from Him. How do we know the right way without hearing? How do we even know the Lord without hearing Him? He's said before that we don't even know what sin is, without the Holy Spirit telling us. So, if you don't even know what sin is without hearing, how do you know how to pray without hearing?

Many times we think we know what we should pray. Yet, have you ever considered that you may be praying for the devil's agenda? If you're not hearing what God wants you to pray, that could be what's happening. This isn't said to create fear in you. However if we don't know what sin is without hearing, how do we know if we're praying into the devil's plan? We must hear, clearly.

Now we know that the Lord's word comes with the power to perform itself. So, if He tells us to ask Him how to pray, then He's going to be faithful to tell us how to pray. In other words, when we ask, we will hear. Just believe.

Today, in your prayer time, ask the Holy Spirit what He wants you to pray. Then by faith, pray that!

Don't pray according to the wisdom of men.

Read: 1 Corinthians 1:19-20　Ephesians 4:14

This devotional study goes with yesterday's in that we need to listen to the Holy Spirit, so we know how to pray. The wisdom of men will get us in just as much trouble as the wisdom of the devil, for the origin is the same.

Ephesians 4:17-18 (NKJV) reads, **"This I say, therefore, and testify in the Lord, that you should no longer walk as the rest of the Gentiles walk, in the futility of their mind, having their understanding darkened, being alienated from the life of God, because of the ignorance that is in them, because of the blindness of their heart…"**.

When we pray according to men's so-called "wise" thoughts and doctrines, our prayers are futile and dark. They are not according to the Spirit.

Allow the Holy Spirit to set the agenda in your prayer life. Allow yourself to listen to Him when praying for people and situations. Many times, people tell us how they want us to pray. We may feel it would be unkind to pray differently from what they tell us. However, God knows best how to pray, not necessarily the person asking you to pray. Always listen. The power of the Holy Spirit will back up those prayers He is directing.

JULY 25

Do pray according to His will and His agenda.

Read: Ephesians 6:13 & 18   James 5:15-18

We left off yesterday saying that the power of the Holy Spirit will back up the prayers He directs. This is true. This is one reason tongues are so powerful. They totally by-pass your mind and are completely Spirit-filled prayers.

Besides praying in tongues, though, we can pray with our minds engaged when we listen to the Holy Spirit and pray accordingly. James writes that the prayer of faith will save the sick. Well, faith comes by hearing. And have you ever noticed how many different ways Jesus healed the sick? He heard and saw what Father was doing and did accordingly. Jesus always prayed according to Father's will and agenda and He had 100% success.

If Jesus is our Master and we are His disciples, this too then is how we will pray. We will listen and look in the Spirit and pray according to what we see and hear.

Command the atmosphere around you to be clear and silence the voice of the enemy. Then look and listen for how to pray today.

JULY 26

Is there another way to have peace?

Read: 1 John 3:21-22   Mark 11:24

When you pray, are you able to let go of what you are asking for, trusting that God has heard you and will answer?

We know, by now, that we need to be hearing when we request things from God. We know that faith comes by hearing, and that when we are praying and are sure God has heard us, we have what we've asked of Him. It's really all based on faith.

Peace, then, comes by faith. For if we know God has heard us, and we have heard Him, we have peace that it will work out as He has spoken to us in prayer. There really is not another way to have peace, than to hear and believe.

JULY 27

What do you really expect from Me?

Read: Hebrews 11:6

When you request something from the Lord, are you expecting to receive what you have requested? When you lay hands on someone for healing, are you expecting healing? When you ask the Holy Spirit to speak to you, are you expecting to hear? When you ask for forgiveness, do you expect He forgives and forgets?

The Scriptures say that without faith it is impossible to please God because those who come to Him must believe that He exists *and* that He's a rewarder of those who diligently seek Him. Do you believe, not only the first half of the verse, but the second as well? Do you believe God will reward you for diligently seeking Him? What are your expectations?

Today, the Lord wants us to seriously consider what we expect from Him when we pray. He wants to answer our prayers. He wants to talk with us. And He wants our expectations to be high. He desires that we expect Him to talk with us, answer us, and lead us. He wants us to expect healing, etc.

Talk to the Holy Spirit today and let Him know what your expectations are. Use the measure of faith God has given you and believe! Pray in faith.

JULY 28

It's His desire to do what people are asking in prayer.

Read: 1 John 3:21-22   Mark 11:24

Today's Scripture readings are the same as two days ago. It bears repeating because the Lord wants you to know that he wants to do what you are asking Him because you are praying according to His will.

John testifies that we have confidence that we'll receive what we've asked of Him because we keep His commands and do what is pleasing in His sight. Well, how do we keep His commands?

Remember we live by the law of the Spirit in the New Covenant. So, His commands are those things He tells us to do. In other words, we listen and obey. And we do those things that are pleasing in His sight means we are doing His will for us. Therefore, one of the things He wills is that we would listen and pray what we hear. If we do that, how can we NOT receive what we've asked for?

Believe you receive and you shall have it! Dare to believe God today! Dare to believe without doubting. He'll let you know if you go too far in your faith, so dare to believe!

Does God inquire of men when He desires to do a thing?

Read: Genesis 18:16-33   Numbers 14:11-20
       Isaiah 1:18   John 15:15

Father asks us, *"When I desire to do a thing, do I inquire of others?"* He goes on, *"I don't need to consult with anyone. My wisdom is the highest and the only real wisdom. However, I enjoy hearing what My sons have to say. I enjoy listening to them and I even enjoy taking into consideration what they desire. When they are My sons, they're one with Me and their desires are not bad."*

We have been learning that it is necessary to listen to the Holy Spirit when we pray. We don't want to pray in agreement with the enemy or against Father's will. However, it is also true that as we listen, we can converse back and forth with the Lord. We can tell Him our requests and ask Him if they're good requests to have.

He doesn't ask foolish questions, and He doesn't ask questions to gain knowledge, but He does love for us to "help" Him. He doesn't really need our help, of course, but He loves it just the same. He loves to hear from us. He loves to hear what we desire and what we think of things. He loves to spend time with us. He loves to take into consideration what we may request. For as He said, when we are His sons, our minds are given over to Him. We've been made new, and the overflow of our hearts is good.

Therefore, don't be afraid to let God know your requests. He may incorporate it into His decisions, especially if He's led you to pray that way.

JULY 30

What is there about prayer that brings joy?

Read: John 16:23-24

Jesus says that our joy in asking for things in prayer is in the receiving what we've asked for. Isn't this true? When we pray for something to happen and it does, there is great excitement, great joy! When we ask the Holy Spirit something and it happens just as He has said it would, there's great joy! It's receiving what we've asked for.

There have been times we've been unable to find something we're looking for. We will then ask the Holy Spirit where it is and He'll tell us and we'll go and look, and sure enough! There it will be! There's great joy in that – it's the receiving what we've asked for. There are other times we've asked Father for something by faith and the joy comes when we receive what we've asked for.

One time I (Tiffany) told God I wanted a muffin and a hot drink. There was a certain kind of muffin I liked to order from a café and the café was closed. The Lord told us to take a walk. We walked and followed the Spirit as He led us in which direction to go. We finally arrived at a coffee shop and went inside. You know what they had? The same muffins that I normally ordered from the other café! And, of course, they had hot drinks also! God is so good.

Father wants us to have joy. He wants to give us what we're desiring. He's not a boring, stodgy old man who's interested in getting us to do a bunch of prayers as some sort of religious duty. He's Life and

He's personal. He's real and He interacts with us. In fact, sometimes Father reserves something specific just for us to pray, to intercede for, and then rewards us for it.

Pray believing you'll receive, today. And go ahead and rejoice in the answer ahead of time!

JULY 31

Do you believe your prayer has power?

Read: 1 Kings 17:1   1 Kings 18:41-46   James 5:13-18

Elijah was a man just like us. In other words, it wasn't that he was so amazing that God answered his prayers. It's that he had faith. He heard God telling Him what to pray, and He prayed it and saw amazing results. We have also learned to listen to God and pray accordingly. It's the hearing God that brings the faith to see the desired result.

It is the just or the righteous, who live by faith. So, when James says that the prayer of a righteous man is powerful and effective, that's a man (or woman or child) with faith!

Elijah had faith. Jesus had faith. All the people in Hebrews 11 (the Faith Hall of Fame) had faith. The Lord has given each of us a measure of faith. Decide you agree with Him that He's given you faith and just believe.

Believe that your prayers are powerful and effective, and you will see things happen.

LOVE AND FAITH

AUGUST 1

My way is the way of love.

Read: John 3:16   John 15:13

If we want to understand the way of love, we need to look at Jesus. He is Love. And He demonstrated what that means. He laid down His life while we were yet sinners! That's incredible. We did nothing to deserve the love that He gave us. And that's not all. He didn't just change our destination, He changed who we are! He has made us born again and given us His same Spirit to dwell in us, making us holy as He is holy, the righteousness of God in Christ. Wow!

Jesus said that others would know we are His disciples by our love. This is true. You recognize others who are in Christ because the same love and the same Spirit that is in you, is in them. God's way is truly the way of love. And love will always make a way to do what is right.

Today, ponder the love of Christ.

AUGUST 2

"The love of God compels me."

Read: 2 Corinthians 5:13-15

Why did Jesus do what He did for us? The answer is Love. John 3:16 says that because God loved, He sent His Son. Jesus came because of love. That same love is now in us through His Spirit.

The Spirit asks, "What is your motivation?" People can be motivated to do things for many reasons: fame, power, money, acceptance, vengeance, pride, lust. The list goes on and on.

For those in Christ, the answer is love. The love of God, not our love, not the world's "love," but the love of <u>God</u>, compels us in all things.

Surrender yourself to His love today.

AUGUST 3

What is Love?

Read: 1 John 4:7-21 NIV   John 15:13 NKJV
1 John 3:16 NKJV

God is love. That simple sentence comprised of three little words is so profound that books could be written about it.

God is love. That means feelings are not love. Words are not love. Organizations are not love. God is love.

And how did God demonstrate love? He came to us in Jesus. He laid His life down in Jesus. He poured out His Spirit through Jesus. He transformed us in Jesus.

God is Love.

Command the atmosphere clear around you. Speak to the Holy Spirit about the question He is asking you today and which Scriptures He has chosen for you to read and ponder.

AUGUST 4

Well done good and faithful servant.

Read: Matthew 25:14-30   Galatians 5:6

The only thing that matters is faith working through love. If you want to hear, "Well done good and faithful servant" when you go to meet the Lord, then this is what you need to do – operate in faith through love.

The phrase, "Well done good and faithful servant," was spoken of those who brought back a return on what was given to them. God has given each of us a measure of faith and love. Use your love and faith together to bring a return on His investment. All this requires is acting on what you believe. To do the works of God is to believe Him. That belief will act by obeying the Holy Spirit.

Therefore, choose love and obedience, and you will hear your Master say: "Well done, <u>good</u> and <u>faithful</u> servant. Enter into the joy of your Master!"

August 5

Pride: Have you reached your goal? Then help somebody else reach theirs.

Read: Luke 17:7-10 NKJV

Love doesn't focus on self. Therefore, don't be concerned about solely accomplishing your own goals. Look to what God has called others to do, and see how you can help them, too.

Was the servant done when he came in from the fields? How long do you work for God? Faith = Obedience. Do you still believe? Then would you still obey and serve God by serving others if they needed help? Love would.

Command the atmosphere clear around you. Speak to the Holy Spirit about this; ask Him to root out any spiritual pride and show how you might help someone else.

AUGUST 6

Jesus: How did He help others reach their goal?

Read: John 14:12   Acts 1:4

When Jesus reached His goal, He poured out everything on us that was His – love, authority, the Holy Spirit, righteousness, etc. – to help us reach our goal. He even said greater things we would do. He wasn't afraid of us doing more than He did. In fact, He said it would bring Him glory if we did greater works.

Be willing to help others go beyond where you have gone and rejoice at their success. Reward will follow you, and that is love.

AUGUST 7

The Kingdom suffers violence.

Read: Matthew 11:12

The long-awaited Messiah has come, the One that John the Baptist prepared the way for. Are you violently in love with the Lord? Love is violent.

Jesus took authority from Satan violently, by force, because of love. You could say that Jesus loves you violently!

Ask the Holy Spirit to burn passion in you so that you love Jesus with a violent love.

AUGUST 8

Love does not act unbecomingly. Do you?

Read: 1 Corinthians 11:17-22 1 Corinthians 13:5 NASB

Sometimes we need to be told what love is like, don't we? It seems obvious, having read or heard the topic for the day, that love would never act unbecomingly.

We can see that the Corinthian church was not acting in love toward one another, can't we? They were really being selfish. Sometimes that's all it takes for us to act in an unbecoming manner. Other times, we feel as though we have a right to act in an unbecoming manner because of how others have treated us or how others are acting. Can you imagine Jesus doing that?

Can you imagine Jesus throwing a fit in the Garden of Gethsemane? He asked his disciples to watch and pray with Him. It's the night He's going to be betrayed and then He's going to be crucified for the sins of the world. And they fell asleep? Twice? Really? Would you think maybe if you were Jesus, you would have a right to let 'em have it? Just let them know that they really failed miserably at the point when you needed the most help? You can imagine what you might be tempted to say to your so-called "friends."

But love doesn't act unbecomingly. We don't see Jesus ever out of control. Even when He overturned the tables of the money changers, it was pre-meditated. He was angry, but not out of control, not unbecoming.

We need to be looking in our spirits and listening with the ears of our hearts to the Lord, all the time. For our responses to situations and people must be like His. And it won't be in an unbecoming manner.

Prayer: Holy Spirit, lead us not into temptation, but deliver us from evil. We give up unbecomingness and choose love. Amen.

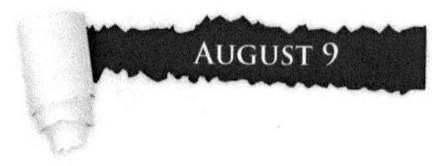

AUGUST 9

Love does not seek its own!

Read: 1 Corinthians 13:5 NIV   Matthew 6:33 NKJV
Philippians 2:3 NIV   Romans 13:14 NKJV

The world tells us, "It's every man for himself" and "You better watch out for yourself, no one else will do it for you!" But when our trust is in Jesus, we no longer need to seek our own good. We no longer need to seek after things for ourselves. We've died to self and now we live to God. If we are dead to self, then we can say, "For us to live is Christ," just as the Scriptures testify.

If we are seeking after our own, then we're really being selfish and living in unbelief about the truth that God works everything for the good of those who love Him and are called according to His purpose.

Jesus tells us to seek first the Kingdom of God and His righteousness and **all** these things will be added to us. So, keep seeking His Kingdom (His way) first and His righteousness first. He'll be faithful to give you what you need, and even what you want, as your heart is lined up with His. He really is good all the time.

AUGUST 10

Are you easily provoked? Love isn't.

Read: 1 Corinthians 13:5 KJV   Matthew 18:21-22
       Luke 4:24-30

Do you have a temper? Are people afraid to tell you things because you might fly off the handle? Easily provoked means you get upset easily. Love doesn't do that. God doesn't do that.

Easily provoked can mean easily frustrated too. In the past I've gotten frustrated easily, but the Lord showed me frustration is really a form of anger, and anger is really a form of hatred. Well, that's certainly not love. So when I feel the temptation to be frustrated, I am reminded that frustration is not from God, and in fact, is definitely from the enemy.

Whether you deal will being easily angered, or easily frustrated, or easily offended, it's really all the same thing. It's easily provoked. That's not love.

In the passages we read, we see that love forgives every time, not that it gets provoked easily. We also see people Jesus spoke to getting easily provoked, provoked enough to try to kill the Lord. Yet, He was not easily provoked in return, but simply walked away.

The Lord isn't telling us this to condemn us, but to correct us because He is conforming us into His image, and He is not easily provoked.

Prayer: Father, I repent of being easily provoked. I choose love instead. I choose to trust You and I am asking for you to give me grace to no longer be easily provoked and no longer believe I have to be. I can love as you do by your power in me. Thank You Jesus! Amen.

AUGUST 11

Love does not take into account a wrong suffered.

Read: Acts 7:51-60   Luke 23:33-34

Love does not take into account a wrong suffered because love forgives. Love holds nothing against someone at all. Look at Jesus. Did anyone ever suffer like He did? He was marred more than any man, the Bible says. He was the only One who never did anything to deserve any suffering whatsoever. If there was ever an injustice done to someone, it was done to Jesus because He was innocent. He didn't deserve to be punished and die. And yet, as He was breathing His last breaths, He asked the Father to not hold the sins of the very people killing Him against them.

Like a good disciple, Stephen too asked for forgiveness for those stoning him. We also are the disciples of Jesus. We, too, can truly overlook a wrong suffered. We, too, can let go of what others have done to us and walk in freedom, not weighed down by unforgiveness and bitterness.

Don't keep a list of wrongs done to you. God doesn't. Forgive, even as God has forgiven you. The power is in you to do it. The choice is yours.

If unforgiveness and offense are something you struggle with, you may want to read *The Bait of Satan* by John Bevere.

AUGUST 12

Love does not rejoice in unrighteousness.

Read: 1 Corinthians 13:6 NASB

Today's devotional topic seemed far-fetched to me, at first. I thought, "Who in their right mind would rejoice in anything unrighteous?" And yet, God felt it necessary to point out to us that love does not rejoice in unrighteousness, or as the NKJV says, "does not rejoice in iniquity." Iniquity is sin.

Look around you and see. How many LGBTQ flags do you see waving? How many parades for "women's rights" as a masquerade for killing unborn children? How many celebrate gay weddings? How many party all night in drunken revelries? How many celebrate sex outside of marriage in TV shows, movies, and real life?

Yes, I think it needs to be said that love does not rejoice in unrighteousness. The world tells us that love accepts everything. It's a lie. Love does not accept everything. It does not rejoice in unrighteousness.

Love died for you that you may become righteous. That's real love.

AUGUST 13

Love rejoices in the Truth!

Read: 1 Corinthians 13:6   Psalm 119:97-104
         Psalm 141:5a   Proverbs 9:9

Love always rejoices in the truth! Even if the truth comes as a rebuke or a correction to us, our hearts rejoice to be in the truth. His love has been poured out in our hearts, and His Holy Spirit leads us into all truth, so even if the truth hurts at first, our hearts rejoice in it.

I'm going to tell you a testimony of a truth that hurt at first, but I rejoice in the truth now. I (Tiffany) have a friend who noticed that I would occasionally make comments about people who had a lot of children. I would say things like, "Didn't they know how to stop that, and why would they want so many?" etc. This friend of mine took me aside, one day, and told me that the Lord had shown her that I was to stop speaking this way. She said that I was someone that people looked up to and making statements like that went against the truth. She said that her young daughter was worshiping the Lord and the Holy Spirit spoke to her and said, "See, you could have had many more children to praise Me." We had been looking at ourselves, what we thought we could handle, what we thought we wanted, etc. We were totally selfish. Once she brought this truth to me – that God loves children and He really meant it when He said, "Be fruitful and multiply" because He considers children a blessing, I cried and cried. I was so upset that I had decided how many children I wanted; I had decided for others what was wise for them to do, etc. However, with that revelation of children, I was also set free. The truth truly sets us free, and I was able to rejoice in that truth.

This is the kind of thing God does. He brings us the truth and our hearts rejoice in it. It will not be painful every time the Lord brings us truth, but even if it is, we will rejoice because His love is shed abroad in our hearts! Amen.

AUGUST 14

Love bears all things.

Read: 1 Corinthians 13:7   Luke 22:54-62

Have you ever wondered if your love is strong enough to bear anything? Perhaps you thought if something really terrible happened between you and a loved one, you couldn't be sure your love would make it. Maybe a situation between you and your spouse, or a situation between you and your parents, or your children, or someone else.

Do you know that love actually bears all things? Love is not breakable. It doesn't break under a heavy weight.

Remember when Peter denied Jesus three times on the night of Jesus' arrest? Did Jesus' love for Peter break under that heavy weight? Peter was one of Jesus' closest friends. He was part of Jesus' inner circle. What would you do if one of your closest friends denied you at your darkest hour? In fact, he didn't even pray for Jesus when He needed it. Would your love bear it?

Love bears all things. It doesn't break under pressure. Remember that the next time the enemy tries to tell you that "it's too much and you just need to quit," or some other lie that implies your love doesn't bear all things.

AUGUST 15

Love believes all things.

Read: Acts 17:10-12   Galatians 5:6 NIV

The Bereans listened to Paul and Silas in faith because love believes all things. This is why they searched the Scriptures with all "readiness." They were ready to believe because love believes.

The only thing that matters is faith expressing itself through love. Well, that's because love will believe. And 1 Corinthians 13:13 says that these three remain: faith, hope, and love. But the greatest of these is love. That's right, because love will believe. Jesus said if you love Me, you will obey My commands. Yes, because love believes, and obedience means you are believing what He is saying.

In other words, when you hear something from the Holy Spirit, believe first in love, and then ask for understanding, like the Bereans did.

Love truly believes all things. Allow your heart to believe. If you've heard God wrong on something, the Holy Spirit will correct you. He's looking for you to believe, and your open heart of love will believe all things.

AUGUST 16

Love hopes all things

Read: 1 Corinthians 13:7   Colossians 1:27
       Zechariah 9:12 NKJV

How can you be a prisoner of hope unless you believe in the love of God? Jesus in us is Hope. So, is it any wonder that love hopes all things?

When we believe the things God has said, we become prisoners of hope. And we believe Him because we love Him and are assured of His love for us.

That hope is in you in Christ Jesus. That hope is part of the love that is now part of you. Love hopes all things.

Blessing: Now may the God of hope fill you with all joy and peace in believing, that you may abound in hope by the power of the Holy Spirit. (Romans 15:13)

AUGUST 17

Love endures all things.

Read: 1 Corinthians 13:7   1 John 4:7-8 & 16

Similar to "love bears all things" from the other day, it is true that love endures all things as well. As always, we look at Jesus. Look at what He bore. We discussed how He bore the burden of praying alone in the Garden – everyone else fell asleep.

We can see He also bore alone the knowledge of the one who would betray Him. Even when He told the disciples at the Last Supper that it was Judas – the one who He gave the piece of bread to – they didn't get it until later when they saw Judas actually betray Him. Jesus really bore things alone for the most part.

Yet, His love endured. He did not give up when it was hard, when people He came to save said He did miracles by the hand of the devil, when they called Him a blasphemer, spit on Him, mocked Him, tried to kill Him, and then eventually really did kill Him. His love endured all things. There was nothing that could stop Love. Nothing. Love endures all things.

That love is in you. Declare with us, that your love endures all things because God is Love, and God is in you!

AUGUST 18

Love NEVER fails.

Read: Jeremiah 31:3   1 Corinthians 13:8a & 13

Love never fails. This then is the key to real success. If you want to live without failing, choose love. The power is in you by the Spirit of the Lord to choose love. The love is in you.

Similar to choosing to forgive or choosing to believe, all you need to do is choose to love. Reject pride, reject offense, reject opinions. They all are contrary to love. Instead, choose love. You will never fail.

Even faith is found in love because Jesus said that those who obey Him are those who love Him. So, if you have love, you have it all and you will not fail!

AUGUST 19

Love wins.

Read: 1 Corinthians 12:31-13(NIV)   Galatians 5:6 (NIV)

When God tells us what the greatest thing is, we should pay attention. In 1 Corinthians 12, Paul is writing to the church in Corinth about spiritual gifts, which he tells them they should earnestly desire. But before he continues writing about those gifts, he inserts a chapter on love, telling the Corinthians that the gifts he's teaching them about are worthless without love.

In fact, as we read in Galatians, the only thing that counts is faith expressing itself through love. Jesus said that if we have faith, nothing will be impossible for us, but even faith is worthless without love.

Can you see why we would need love? Can you see how love wins? Can you see how love won at the cross? Can you see why the Scriptures say that it's the kindness of God that leads men to repentance? And this is why when Jesus healed the sick and raised the dead and cast out demons, people repented? They saw the love of God, and their hearts were transformed. Only love can do that. Only love can change people into something completely different.

Therefore, love wins. Love always wins. As Solomon writes:

> ...love is as strong as death, its jealousy unyielding as the grave. It burns like blazing fire, like a mighty flame. Many waters cannot quench love; rivers cannot wash it away. If

one were to give all the wealth of his house for love, it would be utterly scorned. (Song of Solomon 8:6b-7 NIV)

And as we've seen in Christ, love is stronger than the grave. Love has even overcome death. Love always wins!

Prayer: Father, in all things, keep us in love. In Jesus' name, Amen.

Recommended worship song: *You Won't Relent* by Jesus Culture

AUGUST 20

How should differences be settled between a husband and a wife?

A place of disagreement or differences may sometimes be found between a husband and wife. How should those disagreements or differences be settled? Do we compromise, like find a middle ground somewhere? Does the husband get to choose because Paul wrote that the man is head of the wife? If one spouse is in Christ and the other is not, does it make a difference on how they settle differences between themselves?

Read: Luke 14:26   Romans 12:10 (NIV)

In the first verse, we are told to count the cost of discipleship. In the second verse, we're told to treat each other with love. Both are true.

The Lord is looking for followers. He asks, "Does your relationship with your spouse supersede your relationship with Jesus?" The obvious answer is, "no."

If you and your spouse are both in Christ, then settling differences should be quite easy. In Christ, we are dead to self, so wanting something our own way is wrong. Wanting something the Lord's way is right. When there is a difference, stop and ask the Holy Spirit what He has to say. He doesn't have two opinions. God is not divided. If you both hear different answers, check your heart to make sure you're not being swayed by your own desire. Command the enemy to be quiet and ask again. He will speak to you and bring you both into agreement with Him.

If you are married to an unbeliever, one who doesn't listen to God, you are still responsible for listening to and obeying the Lord. Sometimes He may tell you to go along with your spouse in what they are desiring to do. Other times, He may tell you to stand your ground. Either way, be willing to follow.

Prayer: Father, give me the grace to hear you even when I want something different and to obey even when it's difficult. I believe Your word comes with the power to perform itself. So, if you tell me to do something, the power is there to do it. Amen.

How do believers settle disagreements, even when it involves Scripture?

Read: 1 Corinthians 6:1-3   Galatians 1:11-12

Another place of disagreement is between believers. When it involves disagreement on the meaning of Scripture, people often say, "Well, you know, everyone has their own opinion." Well, God also has an opinion, and His is the right one. In everything, we need to agree with Him.

The Holy Spirit wrote the Scriptures through men. He also interprets them through men in the way He sees fit. When Jesus, or one of the apostles, brought revelations out of the Scriptures, the people frequently misquoted or took the Scripture out of context. Or at the very least, the Scripture didn't mean what they thought it meant originally.

Therefore, when believers settle disagreements, they need to be asking the Holy Spirit what He has to say. Settling disagreements will always involve listening, even when it involves Scripture.

The goal is not to "win" an argument, but to come into agreement with the Holy Spirit. You will have to be humble in order to do this. Be willing to submit to what the Holy Spirit clearly reveals, and if He is not clearly revealing the answer, then ask Him what to do about it. You can even bring in another believer to help you, as we read in 1 Corinthians 6.

And remember that revelation for the church comes through the Apostles and Prophets, but mainly the apostles. So go to an apostle, if necessary, especially if the disagreement involves Scripture because, like Paul, apostles receive that revelation from the Lord.

And in all things, treat each other with love because love never fails! (1 Corinthians 13:13)

AUGUST 22

Why do you want to keep going around that mountain?

Read: Deuteronomy 2:1-3 (NKJV)

Some people say the hell you know is better than the hell you don't know. That should never be the saying of one who is in Christ. The Holy Spirit doesn't lead us into hell. He leads us into the Promised Land. How long it takes to get there frequently depends on us.

The Lord tests us and the Holy Spirit leads us into deserts, like He did Israel. However, He doesn't lead us somewhere so we can be defeated. He leads us into victory. But if we continually choose the wrong path, we're going to keep going around the mountain until we finally stand in faith and keep standing! We can best the wilderness with Him!

So, whatever promise He has given you, believe it, regardless of how it looks around you. Determine you're not going to keep going around the mountain. Instead, like Joshua and Caleb, you are going to believe the report of the LORD and not the report of the enemy.

August 23

Lift up your eyes.

Read: Genesis 13:14-16 Genesis 31:4-13
Genesis 22:4, 13-14 John 8:56

In the first two accounts in Genesis above, we see people of faith lifting their eyes, and what did they behold? They beheld the promises, favor, and blessings of God.

Had they not lifted their eyes, what would they have seen? Abraham would have seen Lot take what appeared to be the best of the land. Jacob would have only seen Laban cheating him at every turn. Both could have become downcast and had a case of the "Poor Me's." Instead, they lifted their eyes, the eyes of their hearts, and they saw what God was doing. Both were filled with faith, received heavenly vision, and received what was promised.

In the second two Scriptures, we see that Abraham lifted his eyes and he didn't merely see a mountain. He didn't just see a ram. He saw the day the Messiah would come and redeem mankind. He saw Jesus!

All the promises of God are "yes and amen" in Christ Jesus. When we lift our eyes, we are really beholding the Lord, for it is only through Him the promises come. It is only through Him we can see what Father is doing. It is only through Him we can truly see.

The Lord says to you today, "Life up your eyes! See what I see! See what I am doing! Believe me and not the circumstances! Lift up your eyes! Amen."

HEALING & DELIVERANCE

Were there any demons who didn't bow to Jesus?

Read: Matthew 8:16 Acts 10:38 1 John 3:8
John 17:4

Try as you might, you will not find one instance of a demon not leaving when Jesus told it to. There is an instance where He spoke and kept speaking to the devils until they left the demoniac, but they did all leave. Later, Jesus confessed to Father that He had completed the work Father sent Him to do. This could not be true, if He hadn't been able to overcome a demon.

This, then, is our destiny. If we are as Jesus is in this world and all the demons left for him, we can expect all the demons to leave for us, too. Don't get frustrated, upset, or give up! Expect the enemy to leave at your authority. It's the power of God in you that shall accomplish it. Praise Jesus!

AUGUST 25

Where there any sicknesses that didn't leave when Jesus touched someone?

Read: Matthew 8:16 Matthew 12:15
Mark 7:24-30

Similar to yesterday's devotional, we must understand that all authority in Heaven and on Earth has been given to us so that we can go in the authority of Christ. And we've been given the same Holy Spirit that raised Jesus from the dead to dwell in us. So not only is authority given, but power as well.

As noted in the Scripture above, even when Jesus wasn't called to a particular area, He still healed the sick and cast out demons. It is God's will to heal, so go after sickness with the same intensity you would go after sin. Don't tolerate it. Believe God and expect healing! It is recorded repeatedly that Jesus healed *all* who came to Him. There's not one sickness that didn't leave when He commanded it to. Expect the same in your life; for as He is, so are we in this world.

God bless you!

AUGUST 26

Can any Spirit-filled man, woman, or child cast out a spirit (demon)?

Read: 1 John 4:4

When you are filled with the Spirit of Jesus Christ, then He who is in you is greater than he who is in the world. This is true, regardless of age or sex. The power to cast out a demon comes from the Spirit of God. The authority to cast out a demon comes from Jesus. When you are filled with the Holy Spirit, you have both authority and power.

Therefore, don't be intimidated by the powers of darkness. Remember that He who is in you *is* greater than he who is in the world. And it's He who is in you who does the works!

AUGUST 27

How do I know if a spirit needs to be cast out?

Read: John 5:19   Luke 11:14

How did Jesus know a spirit needed to be cast out of the mute person? How did He know it wasn't some defect with the vocal cords or something else that needed to be fixed?

The answer is in John 5:19. Jesus couldn't do anything, except what He saw His Father do. If we are His disciples this is how we'll also operate. We'll "see" what Father is doing, and we'll do that. In other words, we'll be listening to the Holy Spirit and looking in our spirits to see what He is doing. Then we'll do that.

Jesus knew the mute person needed a spirit cast out because that's what He saw Father doing. He saw it by the Holy Spirit. Jesus sent us His same Spirit, so we too can do as He did.

August 28

Do I have to know the name of the spirit in order to cast it out?

Read: Mark 3:10-11   Mark 7:24-30

Any spirit of the devil is unclean. In these two instances from history, we can see that Jesus did not name the specific name of the spirit, He simply cast them out. For the one, He called it unclean. For the other, Mark described the spirit as unclean, but Jesus called it a demon.

If the Holy Spirit is bringing the name of a spirit to you, then use the name of the spirit to cast it out of the person. Or, if the Holy Spirit prompts you to ask for the name of the spirit, either from the Lord or from the spirit, then ask the Lord, or command the spirit to tell you. Then cast it out.

Some of the more common names may include: a spirit of fear, a spirit of infirmity, a jezebel spirit, a spirit of rejection, the spirit of death, or the spirit of cancer, etc. You don't have to study up on what kinds of spirits there are (unless, of course the Holy Spirit tells you to). You only need to listen and follow what you hear.

Therefore, it's really only necessary to know the name of the spirit if the Holy Spirit is telling you or leading you to know it. Otherwise, just cast it out.

AUGUST 29

What if I think there's a spirit to cast out, but there really isn't?

Read: Romans 8:1

If you think there's a spirit to cast out and there really isn't, what will happen? Nothing. A spirit won't leave because there isn't one there!

Is God going to be mad at you because you got it wrong, trying to cast out a demon when there wasn't one there? No. Are you trying to follow the Holy Spirit? Are you trying to do the works of God? Are you a soldier in His army who took a shot and missed? Would He be mad at you for trying? Of course not. You reload your gun and try again.

Besides that, you'll learn to recognize His voice even better each time you try. So, don't worry about failing. You can't fail in Christ. You just get back up and try again.

AUGUST 30

What, exactly, do I say to cast out a demon?

Read: Matthew 8:16   Luke 4:35   Mark 5:8

Matthew 8:16 says that Jesus cast the demons out with a word. That's not saying much – like, maybe He just said, "Go!" But then in Luke 4:35, Jesus said, "Be quiet and come out of him!" And in Mark 5:8 Jesus had to repeatedly say, "Come out of the man, you unclean spirit!" And if you remember our reading from a couple of days ago, Jesus didn't say anything to the demon when He cast it out of the Syrophoenician's daughter. (Mark 7)

That's reminiscent of another believer we know who just hugged a young lady until all the demons left her. Just the power of faith and love working together, and she was completely delivered.

But, don't we at least need to say, "In the name of Jesus"? When we're operating in the name of Jesus, it's not just a name we throw around like a magic formula. It's who we are. We go in the name of Jesus. We operate in the name of Jesus. We live in the name of Jesus, love in the name of Jesus, heal in the name of Jesus. We don't even have to use His name all the time because He's actually in us doing the work through His Spirit!

Don't worry about if you'll say the right thing. Just listen and obey out of love. You'll look behind you and see the miraculous at work, including the casting out of demons.

AUGUST 31

How could the discerning of spirits gifting help in casting out a demon?

Read: Acts 16:16-19

The gift of discerning of spirits is simply to know whether or not a spirit is of God or not. There's the Holy Spirit and the angelic spirits who are from God. The demonic spirits are of the darkness. When you discern spirits, you are recognizing where the spirit originates from. Many times the Holy Spirit will give the person with this gift the name of the spirit, as well. Sometimes the person discerns through smell, or sight (spiritual or physical), or a feeling, or just a knowing. This is helpful to know what spirit is operating in a certain setting so that using our authority, we can kick out the unwanted spirits.

Remember that the enemy masquerades as an angel in light. He doesn't show up with a red tail, pitchfork, and horns. He looks beautiful and says things that sound right. But it's evil through and through.

How did Paul know this young girl was speaking from an unclean spirit? Was it from what she said? No. What the spirit was saying through her sounded right. But Paul knew through discerning of spirits that it was wrong.

This is also what Jesus did when Peter told Jesus that He wouldn't be killed or tortured. Instead of saying, "Yes, Peter, I don't think

God would want something bad to happen to Me. I mean, I'm His only begotten Son after all," Jesus said, "Get behind Me, Satan!" He discerned that though what Peter said sounded nice, it was not of God. It did not originate from the Father.

The gift of discerning of spirits is very helpful, then, in casting out demons. You have to know if there's one there to cast it out, right? So, ask the Holy Spirit for this gift. And even ask for the gifting in such a great way that you know what kinds of spirits are operating. It takes much less time if you just know what's going on and can get rid of the spirit, right away.

SEPTEMBER 1

What was Paul's thorn in the flesh?

Read: 2 Corinthians 11:22-33, 12:7-10
        Numbers 33:55

Many people have ideas of what Paul's thorn in the flesh was. Most often people like to say that it was a sickness. Then they can say that God doesn't always heal. However, that thought is contrary to Scripture and the atonement of Christ.

From the Scripture we just read, we ought to be able to see what Paul's thorn in the flesh was. While it is possible that Paul had trouble with his eyes (from Scriptures like Galatians 6:11 and 4:13-15), this is not what he was referencing as a "thorn in the flesh."

First of all, the word "infirmity" used in these verses means "weakness." It doesn't even mean sickness or infirmity.

Secondly, the Bible tells us that thorns in the flesh are those who are attacking us, whether spiritual or physical (Numbers 33:55). Well, from what Paul tells us he endured in persecutions, that would make a lot of sense.

Almost everywhere Paul went, the enemy was inciting people to beat him up and try to kill him, which is in line with what the LORD told him - that he would suffer for Christ. Acts 9:16 says, **"For I will show him how many things he must suffer for My name's sake."** This is also why Paul knew that he still had more suffering to endure when he said in Colossians 1:24, **"I now rejoice in my** sufferings for you, and fill up in my flesh what is lacking in the afflictions of Christ, for the sake of His body, which is the church...".

Therefore, when Paul asked to have the thorn removed, the Lord said, "no," because He had already told Paul he would have to suffer. Sickness was paid for at the cross, but we do have to endure suffering for the name of Jesus, at times. And yet, as Jesus told Paul, His grace is sufficient for us!

DISCIPLESHIP

As He is, so are we in this world.

Read: 1 John 4:17

We've been so indoctrinated in religion that we have frequently bought into the mentality that only leaders are supposed to be disciples with all authority. However, it's not just leaders. It's all of us. We're each as He is in this world. To be a disciple is to have all authority. We can't expect leaders to represent us in this. Instead, each of us is to represent Him – Jesus.

Command the enemy to be silent and removed from your presence. Then ask Jesus to show you how He is. Not how He was on earth, but how He is.

SEPTEMBER 3

What does it look like to be as Jesus is in the world?

Read: Matthew 28:18-20   1 John 3:8b   Acts 10:38

The above Scriptures give us a hint of what it looks like to be as Jesus is in this world. The Bible further states in Ephesians 3:10 that the church is to make the manifold wisdom of God known to the principalities and powers in the heavenly places.

In other words, we are to bring Jesus to earth. We are to establish His Kingdom on earth. We do this by breaking the powers of darkness, tearing down strongholds, releasing healing and deliverance, and more!

Ask the Holy Spirit today to empower you to be Jesus in the world. Listen for Him to guide you today. Then boldly obey what you hear.

SEPTEMBER 4

Did the devil ever win against Jesus?

Read: Ephesians 1:22   Matthew 4:1-11
       Colossians 2:15   Hebrews 2:14

Jesus repeatedly bested the devil at every turn. As we read in another day's devotional, Jesus completed the work Father gave Him to do. This included defeating death and the devil. It is impossible for God to lose. He doesn't even have thoughts of that.

As disciples of Jesus, as those who represent Him in this world, we, too, do not have to accept defeat against the enemy. We can expect to win against the enemy, every time. And the Lord says we will always win if we don't give up.

SEPTEMBER 5

All authority has been given to Me – so GO!

Read: Genesis 1:27-28   Matthew 28:16-20

In the beginning man was given authority by God, but as we know, Adam gave his authority to the enemy. However, when Jesus came as a man, he took authority back from the enemy and gave it back to man. Now all authority in Heaven and on Earth has been given to us by Jesus to have dominion, once again, in the earth.

Therefore, our mission is as Jesus said – to make disciples of all nations, teaching them His commands, and baptizing them in the name of the Father, the Son, and the Holy Spirit. He is with us always, never leaving or forsaking us.

We do not go out on this mission of our Lord's without authority, but with all authority. We teach people what it means to be a disciple of Jesus, what it means to listen to the Holy Spirit and follow Him. We also teach what it means to have the Law of the Spirit written on our hearts and on our minds. And what it means to walk in power as Jesus tells us in Mark 16 (healing the sick, raising the dead, casting out demons, etc.). As we destroy the works of the devil, we establish the Kingdom of God in power and in all authority.

Since Jesus has accomplished what He came here to do, we now have this authority to do as He has done.

SEPTEMBER 6

*Freely **you** have received, freely give.*

Read: Matthew 10:7-8

Yesterday we learned that all authority has been given to Jesus and now to us to go in His stead. Because we have been freely given all things in Christ, we are to freely give what we have been given. As Jesus told His disciples in the beginning, so He says to us, **"Heal the sick, cleanse the lepers, raise the dead, cast out demons. Freely you have received, freely give."**

We've freely been given authority and power to do these things; and we are to freely give what we have been given to set others free and bring them into the Kingdom of God.

Have you been healed? Heal others. Have you been set free from demons? Set others free. Have you been shown the path of Life? Show others. You have been freely given all things in Christ. So, freely give to those around you! And don't worry about failing. God isn't concerned if you'll fail because He never fails and He is with you. So go!

SEPTEMBER 7

Don't throw your pearls to pigs.

Read: Matthew 7:6 NKJV

In the past, the Holy Spirit has shown us this verse to mean that we're not to give our revelation to just anyone, for they may not appreciate it; and in fact, may turn against us, even violently.

But today, the Lord says, He wants His people to know that He doesn't want us to do our best work for something that is not Him.

For example, some people give the best of themselves to their jobs, or their hobbies, or even their families. They may give their best work to their church or a volunteer position. Before we give our best work to these things, good though they may be, we need to know if we're following the Spirit regarding what we are doing.

What has the Holy Spirit told you to do? Is He telling you to work 60-80 hours a week so that you can retire at a certain age and take good vacations in the meantime? Is He telling you to spend 30 hours a week on your hobby or put your kids in travel teams for sports, so you are gone every weekend? But, you can say – "I'm giving them a good life!" Success in life then is based on the number of vacations and sports we give to our kids. Is this what God is saying?

He counts success by following the Spirit. And He counts maturity by Christlikeness. Jesus followed the Holy Spirit and did His best work for Father. That is what Father is telling us to do, today.

Command the atmosphere around you to be clear from the enemy and ask the Holy Spirit about this.

SEPTEMBER 8

Through trials and tribulations journey with Christ.

Read: James 1:12 NIV   1 Peter 5:10 NIV

Have you ever stopped to think about all the trials and tribulations Christ went through? He was opposed at almost every step He took. From the moment of His conception, He was in danger. The earthly father God chose for Him wanted to divorce His mother. Then there was no place to give birth to Him, except in a cave with animals. Then Herod tried to kill Him by murdering all the boys aged 2 and under. The list goes on and on, until finally He gets baptized in the Jordan and the Spirit of God comes upon Him. Immediately the Spirit leads Him into the desert to be tested. From there the opposition came almost every time He opened His mouth or performed a miracle.

Father allowed Jesus to go through trials. Do you think you won't have to? The Bible says no student is greater than their master. If our Master went through trials and tribulations, we will, too. As we do, we will begin to know Him in His sufferings. When you experience something with someone, there is a bond that cannot be made another way. If you go through trials and tribulations with Jesus, you will become closer to Him.

Command the enemy to be silent and ask the Holy Spirit about these things.

September 9

Suffering teaches obedience.

Read: Luke 22:39-46   Hebrews 5:7-9 NKJV

We know that Jesus prayed according to the way Father told Him to pray because Jesus only spoke what He heard Father saying. Yet, Father did <u>not</u> take the cup of suffering from Jesus. Jesus learned obedience through what He suffered. He resisted the lies of the enemy to point of shedding His blood.

It's very easy to say you believe when things are going well. It's very easy to obey the Lord when it's something that you want. But when you are required to keep believing when things are not going well, or when you are required to obey when you do not want to, that is the real test. If we can still believe, still obey when we are suffering, we will learn true obedience. And Jesus said, "If you love Me, you will obey Me". Obedience is a measure of love.

Jesus didn't escape suffering, and you won't either. Each one's suffering may look different, but we will suffer. When we suffer, it tests our faith and our love. Will we keep believing even through the suffering?

Talk honestly with the Lord about this topic and listen to His responses to you.

SEPTEMBER 10

Suffer for doing good and not evil.

Read: Matthew 5:10-12   1 Peter 3:13-18

Jesus and Peter both testify that when we suffer for righteousness' sake, we are blessed. Suffering for doing good is part of the walk of a disciple of Jesus. It is to be expected. In fact, Paul writes in 2 Timothy 3:12 that all those who desire to live godly [like God] **will** suffer persecution.

However, the Lord wants to make a distinction here because there are things Jesus paid for that you do not have to suffer. He paid for your sin. You do not have to suffer for your sins. He paid for your sickness and your freedom from oppression and your peace. You do not have to suffer sickness, oppression, or anxiety (stress). Look at Isaiah 53:4-5 if you need confirmation from Scripture regarding this. The enemy will try to bring these things on you, but you don't have to receive them.

But suffering persecution? Yes, that you will do.

Ask Jesus for grace to suffer for His name in joy. Speak to the Holy Spirit about your concerns regarding this and listen for His response.

September 11

Suffering for Christ is NOT the fate of the unfortunate.

Read: 1 Peter 4:12-19 NIV

Have you ever thought that those who are suffering must have done something wrong? Have you ever wondered if you did something wrong when you suffered persecution? Does this passage shed a different light on the subject for you? The Lord says the reward for suffering is glory!

The Lord wants us to get it in our hearts that it is not the fate of the unfortunate to suffer for Him. Instead, it's a badge of honor to suffer for the name of Christ! Praise God if you are persecuted for righteousness' sake! Praise God if you suffer for being a Christian because you bear the name of Christ!

We have to get away from fear of suffering for the sake of the gospel. There is no fear in love! If we are dead to self, fear has no hold on us. When we come to Christ, part of counting the cost is knowing that you now have a target on your back. A true disciple will suffer for the Lord. But the reward far outweighs the pain. Rejoice!

Command the atmosphere to be clear around you and ask the Holy Spirit to speak to you about the reward of suffering.

Look to the reward!

Read: Acts 9:10-16   Colossians 1:24   Acts 21:10-14

In Acts 9:10-16, Paul is told how much he must suffer for Christ. And in Colossians 1:24, he writes that he knows he's not done with the suffering he was told he must endure. You know the graciousness of God when He tells you in advance how much you have to go through! And this is also the reason why when the prophet Agabus came to Paul in Acts 21:11, Paul still went to Rome, despite the warning of suffering. He knew he wasn't done suffering and he didn't need to despair about it because he had been shown how much he would suffer. Yet through it all, Paul kept the reward as His focus. He testified that he pressed on toward the goal to win the prize in Christ. (Philippians 3:13-14)

Jesus, too, looked to His reward. How could He go through what He suffered for us if He didn't have a goal in mind? The Bible records that Jesus knew the end and looked to the reward (Hebrews 12:2). Father is a rewarder and looks to reward you, as well.

Command the enemy to be silent and ask the Holy Spirit to show you the reward today.

Count the Cost.

Read: Luke 14:26-35

Previously, we looked at how Paul counted the cost. The Lord showed him what he'd have to suffer, and even when Agabus came and told him he'd suffer if he went to Rome, he still went. He knew it was his destiny.

The cost of discipleship is everything. You have to lay down your life to follow Christ. You lay down your opinions, your way of doing things, your desire for everything to be nice and easy, your expectations and the expectations of others, etc. You truly must die to self in order to live for Christ.

After reading today's Scripture passage, count the cost with the Holy Spirit. Seriously consider the cost. Then when you are done, if you still agree to serve Jesus, let Him know that you give up everything and you will follow. Finish by asking Jesus for the grace to follow Him to the end!

SEPTEMBER 14

Life and death are in the tongue – Part 1.

Read: Proverbs 18:21

Your words carry power. They have the capacity to build up or tear down. They can bring life or destroy it. And in Christ, your words have authority, as well.

Are your words bringing life or death? Do you curse yourself and those around you without even knowing it? Do you say things like, "I always get a cold in the winter?" or "My eyes are getting so bad as I get older?" or "My kids just won't listen to me?" or "I can't do anything right?" or maybe "This is going to be a hard day?"

If you are speaking things like this, you're prophesying and speaking death over yourself and others. We need to use our words to declare what God says about us, those around us, and the situations we face. We need to use His words to declare over our nations, schools, and communities.

Life and death are in the tongue – Part 2.

Read: Proverbs 18:21

The Lord says in Joel 3:10b, "Let the weak say, 'I am strong.'" Does that sound foolish to you? Why would you say you are strong if you are weak? If you are sick, why would you say, "I don't get sick?" Why if your child is rebellious would you say, "Praise you Jesus, my child listens to Your voice and obeys You!"

Our words carry power, and they actually change the situations around us. We take what we've heard from the Holy Spirit regarding those around us and declare what He says to be so, regardless of what it looks like. Faith doesn't walk by sight. Take sickness as an example. We can fight it. If a symptom comes, like a sore throat, we immediately rebuke the symptom and the sickness and declare we don't get sick!

Jesus said, He only spoke what He heard from His Father, and Father wasn't saying anything that agreed with the devil. We shouldn't either.

Today, ask the Holy Spirit about these things and ask Him to help you with your words so what comes out of your mouth is what He is saying, and not negativity that shouldn't be there.

SEPTEMBER 16

As a man thinks in his heart, so is he.

Read: Luke 6:45

Today's topic is from Proverbs 23:7. *As a man thinks in his heart, so is he.* Yesterday, we learned that our words carry power. Today, we see that those words come from our hearts, and that's why we need to change them.

In Christ, you've been given a new heart. Sometimes you just need a change in behavior to match your new heart. That's what the Holy Spirit works on. He is conforming you into the image of Christ in every aspect.

Therefore, don't be quick to speak if you have issues with this, but pause and listen to the Holy Spirit so that you can train your mouth to start speaking what's really in your heart – words of faith, hope, and love.

You can tell what's in a man's heart by what comes out of his mouth. Therefore, give it all over to Jesus that by His Spirit, He can work in your heart and your mouth, bringing out good, and not evil.

SEPTEMBER 17

The only way you can bear fruit is to be connected to the vine.

Read: John 15:1-11

Jesus is likened to a vine because He is the Tree of Life. When we eat of the Tree of the Knowledge of Good and Evil we will bear bad fruit, just like what we ate. But when we eat of the Tree of Life, we will bear good fruit, just like that Tree provides.

So what does it mean to abide in the vine? Or to eat from the Tree of Life? Well, look at verse 10 from John Chapter 15. Jesus says, **"If you keep My commandments, you will abide in My love, just as I have kept My Father's commandments and abide in His love."**

When we talked about the Tree of Life, we said you always had to put the Holy Spirit first. Or you could say, you always have to defer to the Holy Spirit. The fruit you bear in the Vine will be Spirit, so you must be listening to and obeying the Holy Spirit. That's where the good fruit comes from.

Remember that the Tree of the Knowledge of Good and Evil is bad, so it bears bad fruit. Stay away from that. You don't want that fruit. But the Tree of Life bears good fruit. That's the fruit you want to be eating. That comes through listening and obeying in love.

SEPTEMBER 18

Have you chosen the Good Vine?

Read: John 15:1   John 7:17

The Lord has created each of us with a will. We call it "free will." We say this because we are free to use our will to make whatever choices we desire. This is why coercion, manipulation, and control cause people and nations to rise up against tyranny. Everyone desires to be free to make their own choices.

While Father is a good Father and desires us to make the choices that are best for us, He doesn't force us to do so. He may try to get us to "see the light," so to speak, in order to help us in making the right choices, but He will not force us to.

Therefore, He has shown us that Jesus is the only way to have life. He is the only way to have true freedom. He is the only way to have truth. He is the Good Vine. Yet, we must decide to abide in Him, in the Good Vine. We must choose.

SEPTEMBER 19

You must choose.

Read: Joshua 24:14-16

Yesterday, we discussed that Father has given each of us a free will. Everyone reading this devotional has likely already chosen the Good Vine. Yet, each day, we must continue to use our free will for life. Our choices bring about life or death. But in Him, there is only Life.

Therefore, when we choose to follow Jesus, we choose the way of Life. Each time we say "yes" to the Holy Spirit as He leads us, we are saying "yes" to Life. This means that each time we say "yes" to the Holy Spirit, we are saying "no" to the devil and to death.

It's sobering to understand that our choices are life or death. Each one. For there is only One way that leads to Life, and that's the way of Jesus. That's the way of following the Holy Spirit.

SEPTEMBER 20

The human will can be used to achieve greatness.

Read: 1 John 3:22

Many people have used their wills to achieve greatness. George Washington Carver was such a man. He would speak with the Holy Spirit each day and ask for wisdom, ask Him what he should do. Through submitting his will to the Holy Spirit's direction, he invented over 300 uses for peanuts and over 100 uses for sweet potatoes, among other things. Truly, he achieved greatness.

Others have not submitted their wills to God's and yet have achieved greatness on a different scale. Take Napoleon or Hitler for examples. Both used their wills to achieve what they desired, but in the end, it led to death.

The Lord wants us to understand the importance of the human will. Those who use their will to achieve greatness can do it, but those who submit their will to the Holy Spirit can not only achieve greatness on earth, but in Heaven as well.

Talk to the Holy Spirit about the will today, asking Him what He has to say about it.

September 21

The human will can be lied to in such a way as to create doubt and unbelief.

Read: Matthew 4:3 & 6   John 7:2-5

What was the devil trying to do to Jesus in these verses? If you said, "create doubt" or something along those lines, you would be correct. Right before the Spirit led Jesus into the wilderness, He was baptized in the Jordan River by John the Baptist. the Holy Spirit came down on Him, and a voice came from Heaven declaring Him to be the Son of God. So, in every way, the enemy was trying to get Jesus to doubt who He really was.

All the enemy has to work with are lies, and he uses them to try to create doubt and unbelief in us so that we align our wills with his, instead of with the will of God.

Today is the day to break off doubting and unbelief. When God speaks something, we can believe it, and it doesn't matter what it looks like or how long it takes for the word to come to pass. We can use our wills to believe God and resist doubting and unbelief.

Prayer: In the name of Jesus, I break off all unbelief and doubt and I declare your will free! You are free to believe God! You are free because where the Spirit of the LORD is, there is freedom! He doesn't come without freedom. Unbelief and doubt, get out in Jesus' name!

And now talk with the Holy Spirit about giving your will to Him and resisting unbelief and doubt from now on.

SEPTEMBER 22

The human will can be harnessed by hell to be extremely evil.

Read: 1 Kings 21 (especially verses 7, 15-16, 17-19, 23, 25)
       2 Kings 9:30-33

When discussing how the human will can be harnessed by hell to be extremely evil, there are very few who compared to Ahab and Jezebel. They gave themselves over to do evil. Many people suffered in their wake because of this, especially the nation of Israel.

In 2022 at the writing of this devotional, the peoples of the nations are again suffering at the hands of leaders who have given their wills over to hell. These leaders think they're somehow in power, but the Lord says they've been harnessed by hell, which means they are being directed by the enemy. For, the human will can either be given over to righteousness or over to sin. Yet, just as the Lord brought justice to Jezebel and Ahab, so will He bring justice to these leaders, big and small, who have worked with this world system to oppress those He loves. Jesus always wins.

Today, praise the Lord for His justice and mercy. Praise Jesus that He has given you a will to do His will!

SEPTEMBER 23

The human will can be lied to and frustrated to become addicted to virtually anything.

Read: James 1:14-15 Genesis 4:7

Have you ever wondered how people can become addicted to things? How does it happen?

The Lord says it starts with a lie. There's a lie that you need something, something other than Christ to make you whole or feel better. Let's take alcohol, as an example. You feel down and the lie comes that having a drink will make you feel better. You decide to look at the lie. Then you entertain the lie. Pretty soon you've partaken of the lie and put action with it. If you don't repent, the lie is able to get a foothold and you are no longer able to control yourself. You have given your will over to something that now controls you.

It all starts with a lie of some sort that you give your will over to. Only in Christ Jesus can that lie, and that power of addiction be broken.

If addiction is a problem for you, ask the LORD to set you free today. Tell Him you don't want it anymore, not even a desire for it. We stand in agreement with you as you do this in the name of Jesus!

SEPTEMBER 24

Anyone who wills to do My will becomes a new person.

Read: John 8:34-36   Ephesians 5:17

Using our will to do His will sets us free. We can truly be born again as we submit our will to His. In fact, this is what true repentance really means. We have chosen to acknowledge that what He says is right and His way is right. We give up our own way and choose the way of the Lord.

Whenever you are tempted to go back to the old way of doing things, meaning your way, remind yourself – even out loud if necessary – that the old man is dead and the new man wills to do the will of the Lord and is truly a new person!

Ask the Holy Spirit today to reveal His will to you, that you may follow Him in all things. Every decision you make, listen to Him today. He will lead you in paths of righteousness – the will of the Lord.

SEPTEMBER 25

If you will to do His will, you're set free to achieve your destiny.

Read: Hebrews 5:5-9

Jesus gave Himself over to do the will of the Father. He chose suffering to fulfill God's purpose for Himself and all humanity. Because Jesus chose the path of the Father, meaning He willed to do God's will, He was set free to achieve His destiny. And as Hebrews says, **"And having been perfected, He became the author of eternal salvation to all who obey Him…"**.

You, too, can be set free to achieve your destiny that will impact numerous others as you will to do the Father's will. In fact, the Bible testifies that apart from God, we can do nothing. Meaning, anything we accomplish apart from following the Lord is worthless and burns up.

Your destiny is found in submitting your will to the Lord Jesus. If there's any area you've struggled with that in the past, let this be the day you choose to give it all up for the will of the Lord and be truly set free to fulfill the awesome plans God prepared in advance for you to do! Amen.

SEPTEMBER 26

I've given everyone a destiny, but they must will to follow it.

Read: 1 Samuel 15

Sometimes, we think we're following our destiny when in actuality, we're following our own desires. Take Saul, as an example. He wanted to be king, as evidenced by his jealousy of David and his fear that David would take the throne from him. God had given Saul a great destiny, and all he needed to do was submit his will to the Lord's and he would fulfill the destiny God had planned for him. But he willed to have the approval of the people more and thwarted what could have been his.

Jesus, on the other hand, never gave in to what the people wanted unless He was shown by the Father to do so. We too, as we will to follow our destiny, must not let anything distract us from what is His best for us. It will affect, not only us, but others as well.

Prayer: Father, give us a will to follow the destiny you have planned for us.

SEPTEMBER 27

A person's destiny which I have given them is what they've always longed for or desired to do.

Read: Mark 5:1-20

A person can be living a life completely outside of Christ, and yet within them, all they want is Jesus. They don't even know that's what they want. They probably don't even understand that their destiny is different from where they are and where they are headed. But inside each of us, God has put a desire in us to fulfill a purpose, a destiny He created for us.

In the account of the demoniac, the man was possessed by thousands of demons, and yet he ran and worshiped Jesus! And then when he got delivered, he wanted to follow Jesus, but Jesus told him to go and tell everyone what God had done for him. He did it and the Bible records that "all marveled." This man was destined to know God and proclaim the testimony of Jesus. He did it and lives changed.

Inside each of you is a destiny that you long for. If you don't know your destiny, ask the Holy Spirit to reveal it to you.

Prayer: Father, I praise you for the destiny you've created for me. I want to fulfill it. Reveal it to me by Your Spirit in the name of Jesus, Amen.

September 28

The longer a person is on a deviant path, the harder it is to come back to the correct course.

Read: Luke 10:13-14

In this account, we see that the cities of Chorazin and Bethsaida were hardened to such an extent, that even though mighty miracles were done in their midst, they still wouldn't repent. We could say they were, as a whole, on a deviant path. The Lord said other cities would have repented had the same miracles been done there.

In our pride, we can get so hardened to sin's deceitfulness that we have a very difficult time coming back to the path of righteousness, or the path of our true destinies.

Jesus is calling each of us into our destinies. These destinies can be fulfilled only in Him, but the longer we resist, the harder it will be to turn to Him.

We are responsible for the revelation that we receive. In the parable of the talents, the people were responsible for what they were given. The cities in the reading for today were also responsible for what happened in their cities. The miracles were done there, but they still didn't repent.

We're responsible, too. What has God done to show us the path of righteousness? What has He done to show us our destinies? What are we going to do with what He has done?

Talk to the Holy Spirit about these things today and give over your will to Jesus.

September 29

I give some over to their own desires.

Read: Romans 1:20-32

The power of a surrendered life cannot be overestimated. For a life that is surrendered to God's design is one in which He rules, and one that is filled with His grace, His empowerment.

However, some refuse to surrender their will to the Lord's design, His destiny for them. And after a time, He may give them over to what they desire. This is what happened to Pharoah in Moses' day, and it's what is referred to in Romans 1:28 from our reading today.

Jesus desires all men to be saved; that's what He paid for. However, He won't force it. If we persist in our ways, He may at some point give us over to our evil desires.

So for us, let it be that we surrender to God's design. Let us surrender to the rule of the Holy Spirit in our lives. Let Jesus be King over us and not self. Let us give up our own desires and be filled with the desire of God!

SEPTEMBER 30

Some are so deceived, that in their pride, they can't come back.

Read: Luke 7:28-35

Here we have an example of those who in their pride, can't come back to the Lord. They were presented with the truth through John the Baptist. Then they were presented with the truth through Jesus, Himself, and He acted completely different from John. Yet, the Pharisees and lawyers wouldn't accept either man, nor their messages.

They actually rejected God's will for themselves. They actually decided not to fulfill their destinies for which they were created.

Jesus truly is the only way and His way is the way of humility – agreement with God. Without that agreement, we can't come to Him. Therefore, if this is an issue for you, call on the name of Jesus; He is an ever-present help in time of trouble!

OCTOBER 1

Come back to Me, and I'll come back to you.

Read: Malachi 3:7

God tells Israel to come back to Him and He'll come back to them. They ask Him, how? And He goes on to tell them things they haven't been doing that they need to start doing. In other words, they need to repent for what they've been neglecting and start doing what is right.

Jesus says to us today, that if we have been straying from Him, all it takes to get going in the right direction again, is to come back to Him. He is always faithful. He is waiting and He is not condemning. He holds out salvation, gifts, authority, and power. He is Love and freely gives His love.

Come back to Him; He will come back to you.

If this devotional passage is not for you today, maybe it is for someone you know. Maybe the Holy Spirit is laying on your heart the name of someone who needs to return to Him. Pray for them today. Pray for them to return to the Lord.

OCTOBER 2

Your desire is always for Me. (Some people just don't know it.)

Read: John 21:15-17

Have you ever wondered why Jesus asked Peter three times if he loved Him? Didn't Jesus know if Peter loved Him?

And have you ever noticed that when God asks you a question, it isn't because He doesn't know the answer? The question is for our benefit, not His.

Peter denied Jesus three times before the crucifixion and wept bitterly when he realized what he had done. Do you think he might have doubted his love for Jesus? Wouldn't the questions that Jesus asked, have been for Peter's benefit?

Sometimes, we don't even realize that our desire is always for the Lord. In Peter's case, he needed to know that he loved the Lord. Jesus already knew it. And Father is telling us today that if we have been born again, our hearts are good and our desire is really always for Him. Even if we stumble, our desire is always for Him.

Sometimes the enemy comes and lies to us about the desire of our hearts, but God is assuring us that our desire is always for Him.

As an example, recently Kirk asked me to pray for him that his passion for Jesus would increase because he had spent an entire day seeking after the Lord and didn't really hear too much and was tempted to get discouraged. He thought that the feelings of discouragement meant that he didn't have enough passion for the Lord. However, God had something different to say. He asked Kirk, "How many people do you think seek after Me all day long when they have an entire day free to do as they please? If that isn't passion, I don't know what is."

Prayer: Father, thank You for giving each of us a desire for You. We confess we do desire You. We want to know You better and love You more. We want Your presence and to know Your ways. We love You and desire You! Thank You!

OCTOBER 3

True happiness cannot be found outside My will or desire for you.

Read: Genesis 17:18-19 & 21:8-14

God's will for Abraham was that he would be the father of many nations. As we know, Abraham and Sarah went outside God's will and had a son named Ishmael through Sarah's servant Hagar. Abraham thought that God should use Ishmael to bring about the promises, but God's will for Abraham was not through Ishmael. God's will for Abraham was through Isaac, the son of promise.

Though Abraham sought happiness outside of God's will, or desire, for him, he could not find it. It was through Isaac, God's perfect plan, that Abraham found happiness.

We, too, will not find true happiness outside of God's plan for us. We will always long for what God has planned for us, if we don't follow the path laid out for us, and this is because He has put the desire for our destiny in our hearts. Only in following Him can we find true happiness.

Today, command the enemy to be quiet and leave your presence. Then ask the Holy Spirit if you are on the right path for your destiny. Are you following the path He has laid out for you? If He says, yes, rejoice! If He says no, ask Him to lead you on the right path and be willing to change.

OCTOBER 4

Power forces a decision.

Read: Luke 4:16-30 & 33-37 John 4:39-42
Matthew 16:13-17

The gospel comes with power. If there's not power in the words, power in the actions, power to back up what the speaker is saying, it is not the gospel. Therefore, in whatever way God manifests His power, it will force a decision. You don't have to force someone to make a decision for Christ. The power of God will force a decision.

When someone encounters the power of God, they have to decide. Is what they have experienced from God? If so, what are they going to do about it? Some will choose to live for Jesus. Others will not, but the decision will be made.

Peter chose to believe Jesus is the Son of God after seeing the power. Those in the synagogue tried to kill Him. The power forced a decision in both cases. And the power still forces a decision today.

Ask God for His power to work through you today!

October 5

Spend time with Me. You'll never be disappointed that you did.

Read: Luke 10:38-42   Matthew 14:23

Jesus spent much time alone with the Father. And we see also that He commended Mary for sitting at His feet and listening to Him, rather than trying to do something for Him.

The time we spend with the Lord can never be taken from us. It is in those times that we hear from Him, we receive strength, wisdom, revelation, and become more intimate with Jesus. It's in the time we spend with Him that we get to know our Father better and the Holy Spirit, as well.

He is always revealing Himself to us, but we will truly never be disappointed having spent time with Him.

The Bible says that if we sow, we will reap. So, don't be afraid to just sit at His feet and listen for His voice. He will speak to you and those times of intimacy will bear great fruit. It's in intimacy in a marriage that bears children. And it's in intimacy with the Bridegroom, Jesus, that bears fruit in us, as well.

Today, spend time with Him. You will not be disappointed.

October 6

Stop, Look, Ask & Ask.

Read: Jeremiah 6:16 (NIV)

This verse starts out saying, "Stand at the crossroads." When you are at a crossroads, there is a decision that needs to be made. The Lord is giving us direction on what to do when we need to make a choice.

The next word is "look." The first thing we do is look in our spirit. What do we see? What is God doing? Then we ask. The Lord says to ask for the ancient paths. This is the way of the Spirit. Jesus is the Ancient of Days, and He will lead you by His Spirit on His path.

The next direction is to ask again. It's good to double check with the Lord. So, ask where the good way is. Ask for His best, and then obey. As the Scripture says, **"Walk in it, and you will find rest for your souls."**

Where is the peace, the rest of God? It is in the stopping, looking, asking, and asking, and then obeying. This is really easy to remember: Stop, Look, Ask, and Ask. It's like when you learned to cross the street. You were told – Stop, Look, and Listen. Or, when you were instructed what to do if you ever caught on fire – Stop, Drop, and Roll.

Always begin by stopping. Don't just forge ahead because there's pressure. Saul was under pressure when he was waiting for Samuel and the soldiers started to leave because Samuel was taking too long, so Saul went ahead and sacrificed without him to appease the soldiers. It cost him the throne.

So, remember to stop. Then look, ask, and ask. The Lord is gracious and wants to show you the right way.

OCTOBER 7

Boldness & Faith

Read: Mark 3:1-6   Acts 4:18-31

Faith and boldness work together. We could even say that faith *is* bold. When you believe God, what can stop you?

Jesus purposely called the man with the withered hand forward and healed him in front of everyone on the Sabbath, knowing full well that the Pharisees would seek to condemn Him for it.

Like their Master, Peter and John boldly told the religious leaders they would not comply with their commands, but would follow the Lord. And then they went and prayed for more boldness! And they received it.

When you are filled with boldness and faith, you cannot help but do the work of an evangelist. The darkness is not a deterrent to you, but an attraction because you desire to turn the light on everywhere you go.

Prayer: Jesus fill us with Your faith and boldness that we may do the work of an evangelist! Amen.

October 8

A disciple evangelizes by default.

Read: Matthew 28:18-20   John 4:28-30   Acts 26

A disciple makes more disciples by default. How do they do that?

Well, if you have been born again, you have a testimony. That testimony brings glory to God when you tell it. It lifts up Jesus. Telling what Jesus has done for you, empowers others to receive the same grace you received.

When you see a sickness, your inclination is to heal. When you see someone oppressed, your inclination is to deliver. As you do these things, sharing the truth and walking in power, you will be helping to make disciples of Jesus. It is in the heart of all disciples to evangelize because we all have been changed and we desire to see others change, as well.

Prayer: Father, thank You that I am a disciple of Jesus, and it is the default of my heart to evangelize and make more disciples. Empower me by Your Spirit in the name of Jesus, Amen.

OCTOBER 9

Being a true disciple flies in the face of religion.

Read: Mark 7:1-23   Acts 5:17-18

Being a true disciple flies in the face of religion, and religion will always persecute those who walk by the Spirit. This persecution is because following the Holy Spirit directly opposes the spirit of religion. The Holy Spirit is the Spirit of Life, and religion is the spirit of death.

Religion is based on knowledge. It's all about what you know. It's about your intellect and what makes sense to you.

Disciples of Jesus Christ follow the Holy Spirit and so walk in power. It's completely contrary to knowledge. In fact, much of the time following the Spirit will not make sense. Remember Jesus said to Nicodemus that those of the Spirit are like the wind. You can't tell where they come from or where they are going. It's not something you can figure out, like you can figure out religion.

So don't be upset when religion opposes you. Rejoice! That's what they did to Jesus and if you're His disciple, they'll do it to you, too.

OCTOBER 10

Religion looks in. Disciples look out.

Read: Luke 18:9-14   1 John 3:7-8

Remember that a disciple of Jesus will evangelize by default? This is because a true disciple of Jesus looks out. They are not looking within themselves. That's what religion does.

Religion compares itself to others. Am I better than my neighbor? Do I obey the rules better? What do they do or don't do compared to me? I, I, I, me, me, me.

Those of the Holy Spirit are looking to Jesus because the Holy Spirit exalts Jesus. And Jesus came to set the captives free and destroy the works of the devil. If we have His heart, which we do if we're born again, then our desire is to set the captives free and destroy the works of the devil, as well.

Don't look in at yourself. It's pride. Instead, look out and see what Jesus is doing. Hear what He is saying and then do that and speak that. Amen.

October 11

Power of self or power of God?

Read: Genesis 11:1-9   James 4:6
        Ephesians 1:17-21

God opposes the proud, but gives grace to the humble. When we are looking at what we can do, that is pride. God opposes that, just as surely as He opposed the building of the Tower of Babel.

Religion is proud because it looks to what it can do, rather than what God can do. "Let's fundraise and get money to build a big building. Let's mail out flyers and try to get people into our church. Let's build programs to get the community to come to our building we built and call it 'outreach.'" The list goes on.

Disciples, however, looks to God and what God can do through them. Disciples of Jesus rest on the power of God, knowing that there's nothing they can do, but it's only what God can do through them that will make the difference. Instead of trying in their own strength to build something, they rest in God and just follow His Spirit, knowing that one waters and another plants, but it's God who brings the increase (1 Corinthians 3).

Prayer: Father I give up striving and trying in my own strength to do anything. I surrender to Your Spirit, to Your will. I choose the power of God. I need You. Amen.

OCTOBER 12

A disciple is comfortable with doing the impossible.

Read: Philippians 4:13   2 Peter 1:2-4   Acts 14:8-10

When we are filled with the Holy Spirit, the same Spirit that raised Jesus from the dead, we know that He who is in us is greater than he who is in the world, and our expectation is the impossible. Therefore, we are comfortable with doing the impossible.

With God all things are possible, and we're never without Him when we're in Christ. Therefore, the impossible should become normal. The normal Christian life should be a life where the impossible becomes possible. This is what Jesus demonstrated and this is what His followers in Scripture did and expected to do.

In these days of the Latter Rain, we should expect even more because Jesus said the things that He did we would do and greater things. Therefore, get comfortable with doing the impossible. It's the life you are called to!

OCTOBER 13

Disciples look at what God has to offer.

Read: 2 Peter 1:2-4   Ephesians 3:20-21   Ephesians 4:7

A disciple doesn't look at what he has to offer. He looks at what God has to offer. Whatever it is that God has called us to do, He has given us the power to do it. His word comes with the power to perform itself. So, if He has spoken to us, telling us to do something, then that word of instruction to us comes with power. That's how it works. Where God guides, He provides.

The Lord has empowered us by His Holy Spirit, the same Spirit who raised Jesus from the dead – the exact same Spirit – to do what He called us to do. Therefore, instead of looking at what we can do in our own strength, we need to lift our eyes and look to what God can do. And we know that with God, all things are possible!

Prayer: Jesus, empower us by Your Spirit to do what You desire us to do. We lift our eyes to see what You can do, rather than what we can do. Help us keep our eyes on you. Amen.

OCTOBER 14

Looking at self is illegal for a disciple.

Read: Hebrews 12:1-3   Philippians 1:21
Daniel 11:32 (NKJV)

Can you perform great exploits while looking at yourself? Can you finish strong with eyes on self? Did Jesus take your place and become sin for you so that you could keep living for you?

When we've been born again, our old man is dead. The old man was concerned with self. The new man is alive in Christ. Therefore, it's Jesus we look at and not self anymore. We're no longer concerned with ourselves, because self has died. Who concerns himself with what has died?

Our eyes should always be on Jesus, considering what He has done and living in His victory, day by day. If we catch ourselves looking at self, we need to bring our minds back to Jesus again. He is the One in whom we live, and it's by His Spirit we are alive, for His Spirit gives life to us.

Looking at self is truly illegal for a disciple of Jesus because self is dead; for us to live is Christ!

OCTOBER 15

Disciples believe they can do what their Master does.

Read: 2 Kings 2:14
Matthew 14:28 (and surrounding verses)

Elisha was a disciple of Elijah. He expected to do as Elijah had done, and he did so. Peter was a disciple of Jesus. He expected to do as Jesus had done, and he did so.

The very nature of being a disciple means that we seek to be like our Master in all things. Therefore, we believe we can do what our Master does. We look at the things He did as recorded in Scripture and believe we can do those things. But we also look at what He is currently doing and believe we can do that as well.

Remember that Jesus said He did what He saw Father do and He spoke what He heard Father say. Therefore, we also look in the Spirit at what our Father is doing and we do that.

Believe you can do as your Master does. Jesus says you can and He cannot lie.

OCTOBER 16

Disciples are not greater than their Master.

Read: John 13:16   John 14:12-14

Disciples are like their Master, but they are not greater than their Master. However, it is true that we can <u>do</u> greater things than Jesus did. But what He empowers us to do does not make us greater than Him.

When we do greater works than Jesus did, we are doing it in His name, through the power of His Spirit, the same Spirit that raised Him from the dead. So, who gets the glory in that? He does! It's His power. It's His Spirit. It's His name!

The expectation is that we will do what He has done and more. But just as it's not our works that make us righteous, so it is that our works will not make us greater than the One who sent us either.

OCTOBER 17

Why did the Lord choose the Apostle Paul to minister for Him? (Saul seems like he was really bad.)

Read: Mark 2:13-17   Galatians 1:13-17, 22-24

Have you ever noticed that Jesus doesn't usually use those we would use? Think of when He sent the Prophet Samuel to anoint David as King over Israel. Samuel went through all of Jesse's sons before he got to David. David was the last one Samuel would have considered. He was a youth, small, and a shepherd. He didn't look much like a warrior. Yet, David was the one.

And then there's the twelve apostles that Jesus chose out of all who followed Him. They weren't the cream of the crop, either. Those who were super smart or righteous were already following rabbis. These were the rejected ones, the fishermen and tax collectors, etc.

And now think of yourself. Would you have chosen you? Not me. I can think of a lot of people who would seem to do a better job than me at what God sends me to do. But God loves to use the foolish to shame the wise and the weak to shame the strong. He gets glory in changing someone from the inside out and making them into something new. Everyone can then say, "That has to be God!" This is why the churches rejoiced at the testimony of what Paul was doing. They knew only God could change Paul's heart.

So, rejoice! Jesus has called you as well, and He will be glorified in you as you surrender to Him!

Further reading: 1 Corinthians 1:18-31

OCTOBER 18

Where did Paul learn to minister for the Lord?

Read: Galatians 1:11, 15-21

Paul received His revelation from Jesus, Himself. He also received it mostly in isolation. He didn't immediately go to confer with the other apostles to see what revelation they had. And he didn't go to seminary to be taught by teachers so that he could receive a diploma and earn the name "apostle." Instead, he learned to minister for the Lord in the desert with the Holy Spirit.

Does this sound familiar? It should. What happened to Jesus after He received the Holy Spirit? He, too, was led into the desert. When He came out, He started preaching and healing and performing miracles.

What about your own life? Have you been called by God? Do you know His plans for you? Are you waiting for them to happen? He will always call you into the desert to train you up before He brings you out into the Promised Land.

Therefore, like Paul and like our Master, Jesus, don't be deterred by the desert. Determine to best it with Him! He'll never leave you or forsake you. You're not sent to the desert alone, but with the Helper and Comforter, the One who leads you into all truth!

OCTOBER 19

What kind of resistance should we expect from our enemy?

Read: Revelation 2:10   Mark 9:12

What kind of resistance do we receive from our enemy? About any kind you can think of!

Jesus was tempted, persecuted and even killed by the enemy. The devil hates God and everything God has made. The enemy's job description is to steal, kill, and destroy. So, where you see that operating, that's resistance from the enemy.

Do we need to fret because we're resisted? Absolutely not! The Lord says that we overcome the devil by the blood of Lamb and the word of our testimony and by not loving our lives even to the death. (Revelation 12:11) Paul tells us in Ephesians 6 to put on the full armor of God and stand. And when we've done everything, then stand and keep standing. In other words, don't give up!

We cannot fail in Christ! Jesus has defeated the enemy. So, though you are resisted, don't quit. You'll never lose if you don't give up!

Does resistance increase as we progress in our Christian walk?

Read: Matthew 4:1   Hebrews 5:8

From the get-go, the devil will resist you as you follow Christ. The resistance will progress as we progress. We can see it in the life of Jesus. The devil resisted Him immediately, from birth, but God protected Him. The resistance increased as Jesus was released into ministry, and it kept increasing until He went to the cross. The good news is that resistance always makes us stronger.

Every athlete knows that resistance training is crucial to becoming better. A marathon runner will practice running in all weather, at different altitudes, even practice sprinting intervals, etc. This is all to gain speed and endurance to be able to win races. The same type of attitude is true for all sports. Resistance is necessary to gain strength, and Jesus is coming back for a strong church.

He endured resistance and grew stronger, and as His disciples, we will too. In fact, Paul writes in Romans 5:3-4 (NKJV), "**… we also glory in tribulations, knowing that tribulation produces perseverance; and perseverance, character, and character, hope.**"

Therefore, count it all joy! And remember that as the resistance increases, it only does so because you've become stronger and more able to handle it. That's good news! You're becoming more and more like Christ!

How does religion play into the hands of our enemy against Spirit-filled believers?

Read: Galatians 4:21-23, 28-31

The Lord told us that the spirit of religion is the same as the spirit of death. How true this is! For the Spirit of Christ is the Spirit of Life. Death opposes Life. Religion opposes the Holy Spirit.

Therefore, those with the religious spirit – the religious – will always oppose those with the Holy Spirit. This is what Paul was referring to in the passage we read, today. Those who desire the law play into the hands of the enemy and a religious spirit gets behind those people to oppose those who follow the Holy Spirit, or the Law of the Spirit.

This opposition from the religious is guaranteed if you walk by the Spirit. But, as the Scripture states,

> **Beloved, do not think it strange concerning the fiery trial which is to try you, as though some strange thing happened to you; but rejoice to the extent that you partake of Christ's sufferings, that when His glory is revealed, you may also be glad with exceeding joy. If you are reproached for the name of Christ, blessed are you, for the Spirit of glory and of God rests upon you. On their part He is blasphemed, but on your part He is glorified.** (1 Peter 4:12-14 NKJV)

So rejoice!

Did Jesus have issues with the religious leaders of His time?

Read: Matthew 12:1-2, 9-14, 22-24

Yesterday, we learned that if you follow the Holy Spirit, you will be opposed by those with a religious spirit. Today, we're looking to see if Jesus had issues like this. From our Scripture reading, it's pretty obvious that He did. In just one chapter of the Bible, there were three separate instances of the religious leaders in Jesus' day opposing Him. That's incredible!

Because Jesus walked by the Spirit, He was opposed by those with the religious spirit. Religion of the world is based on man's ability to reach God. True Christianity says man cannot reach God, so God reached Him. It's very humbling to say that you cannot do anything that's worth anything good in God's eyes; except by the power of His Spirit in the name of His Son, Jesus. There's no other way.

Jesus did everything by the power of the Holy Spirit. When Jesus healed, He did it by the Spirit of God. When Jesus cast out demons, He did it by the Spirit of God. When Jesus allowed His disciples to pick grain and eat it on the Sabbath, something that was forbidden by the "law," He did it by the Spirit of God. In all things He followed God by following His Spirit.

The leaders of Jesus' day followed the law and so everything was based on their ability to follow the law. To follow the Holy Spirit then was an affront.

The same is true today. You can use a search engine to look up any well-known Spirit-filled believer and they will have one, if not many people, whose sole aim in life is to try to discredit everything they do. Jesus went through it, and His believers today still go through it. It's an honor to be counted worthy to be persecuted for His name!

OCTOBER 23

Why do the religious have issues with Spirit-filled believers?

Read: John 9:1-34   1 John 2:18

We've been discussing how those with a religious spirit will persecute those who are filled with the Holy Spirit. But why do they do this?

One reason we mentioned is that the religious spirit is the same as the spirit of death. And death opposes life. Holy Spirit is the Spirit of Life.

Another reason the religious have issue with those filled with the Spirit of God is because the religious spirit is an anti-Christ spirit. It is against Christ. It may masquerade as "Christian," but if it is in opposition to the Holy Spirit, who is the Spirit of Christ, then it is anti-Christ, no matter what it calls itself.

As an example, there was a woman we know who attended a Spirit-filled church. Her husband wouldn't step foot in the church, though he called himself a Christian. He would only attend his denominational church that he was raised in and wanted nothing to do whatsoever with the Holy Spirit. A friend of ours asked this woman, "Well, what doesn't he like about this church? Jesus?" The answer is, "Yes." He would never say he didn't like Jesus. But do we understand that the Holy Spirit is God, and He is called the Spirit of Christ? If we don't like the Holy Spirit, we don't like God. If we don't like how the Holy Spirit works because He's not something we can manage or control, then we have a religious spirit and need to repent.

The religious will always have issues with those of the Spirit because that religious spirit opposes Christ. This is exactly what we see in John 9. Jesus heals a man born blind by the power of the Holy Spirit, and they will not accept that He comes from God. They still insist He's a sinner and that the guy He healed is a sinner too! It's incredible. But if they were to admit that Jesus is the Son of God, they would then have to change what they believe, and that's called humility. So instead, they continue in pride, persecuting those who walk in the freedom of the Spirit.

Today, praise Jesus that you are counted worthy to be harassed by the enemy because you carry in you the Spirit of the risen Christ!

OCTOBER 24

How are we, as Spirit-filled believers, supposed to deal with this persecution?

Read: John 5:19   John 12:49   John 8:37-47
Matthew 27:12-14

The beginning of our Scripture reading for today gives us a basis for how we are to act in every situation, persecuted or not. We need to see what God is doing and do that and hear what God is speaking and say that. With that as our foundation, then we can see how Jesus responded to persecution from the religious.

In the passage in John, Jesus hit the accusations head-on. He told the religious leaders they were sons of the devil because they wouldn't listen to God. Instead, they think they worship God, but with their words and actions, they follow the devil.

In the passage in Matthew, we see that Jesus didn't answer any of the accusations placed against Him by the religious leaders. He was silent and took the beating, etc.

Both of these instances were following the Holy Spirit. This is why it is imperative to be hearing God. We need to see and hear in the spirit and follow what God tells us to do and say. What He told Jesus to do in one instance, He totally changed the next time. If we want to walk in the power of the Holy Spirit, this is how it must be for us, too. We have to be open to God changing it up for us, and in all things, we must stay free of offense, just like our Master.

Praise Jesus for giving you His Holy Spirit today who will lead you in paths of righteousness, so that even when you're persecuted, you know how to respond.

OCTOBER 25

Religion argues. Does the Spirit argue back?

Read: John 7:25-31

If Jesus wanted to enter into arguments with the religious, wouldn't He have told them He was born in Bethlehem? Wouldn't He have called His mother over and had her testify to them about His birth, and the arrival of the angels and the wise men with their extravagant gifts? Instead, He answers by the Spirit of the Lord, which shuts up the religious, but causes faith to rise in those who are not of the religious spirit.

Read: Matthew 21:23-27

In this passage, Jesus refuses to answer their argument about His authority. They're seeking to be critical at every point, and He shuts them down by answering by the Spirit. You'll notice that Jesus frequently asked them questions after they questioned Him. Doing this turns it back onto them instead of causing Him to feel a need to defend Himself.

Read: Matthew 22:23-33

In our last example, Jesus again doesn't argue, but He shuts down their argument against Him that there is no resurrection. He shows them they don't know the Scriptures, nor the power of God. Wow! If He had answered by the letter, or the law, He would have been trapped into an argument.

When disagreements arise, don't argue by the letter, but answer by the Spirit. There's no need to feel obligated to defend yourself or your position. Just listen to the Spirit and answer whatever you hear or feel led to say.

OCTOBER 26

Practice having faith that words will be put in your mouth.

Read: Luke 12:11-12

Jesus spoke these words and we can see that He practiced what He preached. How many times did the Pharisees, teachers of the Law, Herodians, etc. come to Him and try to trap Him in something He said? He had to rely on the Holy Spirit to give Him the words at the proper time. Each time He answered in wisdom. In fact, most times, He completely shut down their arguments.

The Lord wants us to take the promise He spoke in Luke that the Holy Spirit will give us words to say when we need them. He wants us to believe this and not worry in advance about what to say. There are times He will tell you in advance what to say. But today, He is saying to practice having faith that the Holy Spirit will give you the words when you need them.

And remember, the result is not up to you. You plant, or you water, but God is the one who gives the increase, or makes things grow. You just have faith and believe Holy Spirit will give you what to say when you need to say it.

Prayer: Holy Spirit, we choose to believe you, today. We choose to have faith that You will put the words in our mouths that we need when we need them. We surrender to You and believe You! Jesus will be glorified! Amen.

OCTOBER 27

The right answer is always Jesus.

Read: John 1:1-4, 14   Romans 10:6-8

Yesterday, we talked about trusting the Holy Spirit to bring you the words at the right time. Where does He get those words? He gets them from the Word, Himself. Jesus is the Word of God. And He lives in all who believe in Him!

This is why Paul says we can't say, "Who will go get Christ from Heaven or who will raise Him from the dead?" Instead, we have to believe He is in us; the Living Word is in our hearts and in our mouths – He is the word that we preach. You don't have to go somewhere to find Him. He's in you!

When Holy Spirit brings us the Word, He's bringing us Jesus. Hence, the answer is always Jesus! You need wisdom? The answer is Jesus. You need healing? The answer is Jesus. You need peace? The answer is Jesus. You need hope? The answer is Jesus.

Whatever you need is found in Jesus. This is why we listen to the Lord, even when we pray. Because the answer is in Jesus. This is why we stop, look, ask and ask when we're at a crossroads, making a decision. Because the answer is Jesus.

Like yesterday, simply believe. Believe He is in you – in your heart and in your mouth – because out of the overflow of the heart, the mouth speaks. If He's in your heart, that's what will come out of your mouth!

Halleluiah Jesus!

OCTOBER 28

As a follower of Jesus Christ, you will face perils. So, what does that mean?

Read: Romans 8:35   2 Corinthians 11:26

Strong's concordance, which tells us what the Greek meaning of words are in the Bible, says that the word translated "perils" means "danger."

We've read about some of Paul's perils. But what about Jesus? Since He's the One we follow, we need to see what He says and does.

Read: Luke 4:23-30   Matthew 12:9-14

With just these two examples in mind, we see that they tried to throw Jesus off a cliff and then plotted later on to kill him. No servant is greater than his Master. So, if they did it to our Master, we can expect the same.

Understanding perils is part of counting the cost of discipleship. It may come in the form of persecution. It may come in the form of dangers as you travel, or perhaps hunger, or perhaps sleeplessness. God knows what your perils may be, but that you will face them if you walk with Jesus is certain.

Walking with Jesus is the key, however, because He never loses. And if He's with you, you'll never lose either!

OCTOBER 29

What are vain imaginations?

Read: 1 John 4:1

When you are opposed by religion and/or unbelief, there can be vain imaginations that pop up in your mind. In this case, vain imaginations would be arguments or conversations you have in your mind with someone. It's vain – because it's empty – void of anything concrete. In other words, it's not really happening. It's only happening in your imagination. For example, you imagine what you might say to someone. Or, you imagine how it would have gone had you said something differently to someone. In these sorts of vain imaginations, you never lose an argument. You always win.

But God doesn't vainly imagine. When He gives you thoughts, they are not empty. If He gives you a thought about the future, He is inviting you to see what He sees coming to pass. When He gives you a thought about the past, He is inviting you to see the past through the eyes of the Holy Spirit. There will not be arguments, but wisdom and faith.

Therefore, test the spirit from which your thoughts are coming. Is it from God, or is it from a different spirit? If it's not the Holy Spirit, reject those thoughts of vain imagining and ask Him instead what to think.

October 30

Why would vain imaginations come into your mind?

Read: Ephesians 2:1-3

First Corinthians 8:1 says that knowledge puffs up, but love builds up. When we entertain vain imaginations, it is because we think we "know" the right answer. We're looking at things through the eyes of our dead man – the way we used to be, as Paul writes in the verses in Ephesians we just read. This is rooted in pride.

The dead man is dead when you're in Christ. However, the enemy is going to keep trying to get you to act like him, bringing you thoughts like you used to think. That's not you anymore, however. You don't have to take those thoughts anymore and give them place in your mind. That's the way you used to be, but it isn't the way you are now.

Therefore, since you've been made alive in Christ, don't fall for the vain imaginations rooted in pride, that puffs up. Resist that temptation, and the devil will flee from you. Instead, draw near to God, asking Him to replace those vain thoughts with the truth. He will. And that love will build you up, rather than the prideful "knowledge" that puffs you up.

Ask the Holy Spirit today to help you when your mind wanders to vain imaginations. Ask Him to direct your thoughts to truth and love, which are in Christ.

October 31

Why are vain imaginations wrong for the Spirit-filled believer?

Read: 2 Corinthians 10:4-5

We are instructed to cast down arguments and every high thing that exalts itself against the knowledge of God. Vain imaginations – the arguments you have in your mind with others – exalt themselves against the knowledge of God because they are not God's thoughts.

It is wrong for Spirit-filled believers to give place to anything that exalts itself against the knowledge of God. Either Jesus is Lord or He isn't. Anything we lift higher than Him is an idol. That is why it is wrong to give way to vain imaginations for a Spirit-filled believer.

The Holy Spirit leads us into all truth. Jesus is Truth. Anything less is a lie and needs to be taken captive and made obedient to the knowledge of Christ.

This being said, don't go into guilt if you have vain imaginations. As soon as you recognize what's happening, just turn your thoughts to God instead. One way to do this is to ask Him what He thinks.

I was having a vain imagination in my head recently where I was arguing with someone and I thought, "Wait a minute! I don't have to talk to someone who's not here about this. I'm going to talk to My Father." So, I talked to God about it, and we talked back and forth; and the power of the vain imagination was broken. I was at peace and didn't need to keep thinking about it.

Today, invite the Holy Spirit to speak to you about issues you may be vainly imagining about. Write down what He says if you need to in case you are tempted to go back to vain imagining regarding the same issue. This way you can look back and see what He's already said regarding it.

November 1

Should we ever argue or dispute?

Read: Titus 3:9

From this passage we see that arguing and foolish disputes are unprofitable and useless. This is true for several reasons. For one, those who desire to argue with us have no intention of changing their minds. They are trying to prove their point and want to be heard.

Another reason is that arguing and disputing have to do with the intellect. No one is ever born again by their intellect. Whenever the Pharisees or teachers of the law tried to get Jesus to argue or dispute, He ended it by answering by the Spirit of the LORD. And His answer was always wisdom, wisdom beyond what man could come up with, because He was always going for the heart.

Additionally, arguing is frequently based in legalism and religion. Neither of these have anything to do with real Christianity. To argue about them is truly useless.

And lastly, at least for now, is that the gospel comes with power. There's no need to argue or dispute with people. The Holy Spirit comes with power. It's impossible that He doesn't. Therefore, our faith is based on the power of God and not the wisdom of men.

NOVEMBER 2

Enter His gates with thanksgiving.

Read: Psalm 100:4

Do you have a difficult time entering the presence of the LORD sometimes? Do you struggle to hear His voice? Are the other voices around you louder than God's?

We enter His gates with thanksgiving. When we thank God, our attention is turned to Him – the One from whom all blessings flow. As we focus on Him, the struggle to feel His presence, or hear Him, diminishes. In fact, you'll find that faith rises up as you thank Him.

The power of thanksgiving cannot be underestimated. The door to selfishness is closed when we give thanks, and that means the door to the enemy is closed, as well.

Give thanks to the LORD, for He is good!

November 3

Enter His courts with praise!

Read: Psalm 100   Psalm 98:4

Yesterday, you entered the gates of the Lord with thanksgiving. Today, praise Him for who He is. Even as thankfulness closes the door to the enemy, praise defeats him!

Meditate on who God is as you praise Him. You could try going through His many names, like: King of kings, Lord of lords, Beginning and End, Prince of Peace, Wonderful, Counselor, Lord of Hosts, Lamb of God, Lion of the tribe of Judah, Great I Am, etc.

Give a shout unto the LORD! In the court of a King, you shall see the King!

Praise the LORD!

NOVEMBER 4

Lift up holy hands.

Read: 1 Timothy 2:8

Why would the Lord want us to lift up holy hands? Once, I heard someone say that since we've all been given different fingerprints, God looks down and sees our hands raised and says, "Oh, that's my son, Kirk." Or, "Oh, that's my daughter, Tiffany," etc. It's a beautiful picture.

Yet, do you always feel like lifting your hands? Do you always feel like praising the LORD? Jeremiah 33:11 and Hebrews 13:15 tell us to bring the *sacrifice* of praise. It's a sacrifice sometimes because we don't always "feel" like it.

But if we're led by the Spirit, and not by feelings (think living by faith and not by sight), then praising the LORD when we don't "feel" like it, is something we would do. A way we can show adoration for our LORD is to lift our hands and give Him praise. He's worthy regardless of circumstances or feelings.

Lift your holy hands, and praise Him today!

THE CHURCH

NOVEMBER 5

Can the church be in truth without the Holy Spirit leading it?

Read: John 16:13

The Holy Spirit is the One who leads us into all truth. Nothing else does that. Therefore, wouldn't the church be guaranteed to be deceived without the Holy Spirit leading and speaking? However, it doesn't do much good if the Holy Spirit speaks, but no one obeys, right? Therefore, the church of Jesus Christ is one who submits to the Holy Spirit; submission meaning being in agreement with His leading.

This is also why the church must be in operation according to the way Jesus set it up. He's given His apostles and prophets revelation for the church. This revelation is true doctrine. It's not something man made up because it comes from the Holy Spirit. From there, the evangelists, pastors, and teachers take that truth to the rest of the body of Christ to help build them up that they may do the works God has called them to do.

Without the leading of the Holy Spirit, none of this is possible. And without submission to the Hoy Spirit, none of this is possible, either.

Pray for the church today. Pray for the church to be led by the Spirit of truth.

NOVEMBER 6

The ecclesia is not housed in a building.

Read: Matthew 26:61   1 Peter 2:5
        1 Corinthians 3:16   2 Corinthians 6:16

Today, as the Scripture readings indicate, God no longer resides in a building. He now resides by His Spirit in those who have been born again in the image of His Son. Therefore, how can His body be housed in a building?

What does this mean for doing "church?" Think about all the people on earth who are filled with the Holy Spirit. Anyone who encounters a Spirit-filled believer has encountered the church. They've encountered Christ.

Command the atmosphere clear and ask the Holy Spirit about these things.

NOVEMBER 7

Without spot or wrinkle?

Read: Ephesians 5:25-27   Hebrews 10:22

Is it possible for Christ to present His bride to Himself without spot or wrinkle? How could this be? What does it mean that Jesus sanctifies us and cleanses us with the washing of water by the word? Who is the Word? Jesus, right? And who brings us the Word? The Holy Spirit, right?

This being the case, how can one be holy, sanctified, set apart without the Holy Spirit? So, when the Holy Spirit brings us the word, it changes us. It cleanses us. It is Jesus. It is only through Him, His blood, His words, His powerful Spirit that we could ever be spotless and without wrinkle.

Speak Holy Spirit! Bring to us Jesus, today! Cleanse us! By the Word, tear down strongholds today! We submit to the washing! Amen.

NOVEMBER 8

Apostolic Mandate

Mandate can have several meanings. Merriam Webster's dictionary says that mandate is an official order to do something. Therefore, an apostolic mandate would be an official order from an apostle for the church to do something.

Read: Acts 15:1-29

Here we see an apostolic mandate in the making. It was not a law to keep the new Gentile believers in bondage. But it was an order to help them choose the right way as they learned to follow the Holy Spirit. Apostles, as ones given great authority, have the freedom to mandate by the Spirit of the Lord in governing the church.

Command the enemy to be quiet. Ask the Lord to show you somewhere else in Scripture where there was an apostolic mandate. Don't be concerned if He shows you Old Testament as well as New. Kings frequently had apostolic anointings.

Prophetic Decree

Decree: 1) An authoritative order having the force of law.
        2) The judgment of a court of equity
        3) The judgment of a court.
(American Heritage Dictionary of the English Language)

Read: Exodus 14:13-14   1 Samuel 15:26-29

The Lord says, *"Some prophetic words are not decrees, but when I give My Prophets something to say and they declare it as I have said it, it is a decree. It holds the force of law in the Spirit. It shall be according to the word that I have given them."* This has the idea behind it that some words need to be prayed into, which is why they are not necessarily decrees. But some words are decrees. The Lord bestows authority in His church as He sees fit. That authority is recognized in Heaven, whether or not we recognize it on earth. However, can you see how it benefits us to recognize authority the way the Lord does?

As you listen to prophets from here on out, ask the Holy Spirit to help you to recognize a prophetic decree when they speak, and to give you discernment to know what is of Him and what is not.

NOVEMBER 10

Unity in the Spirit among the five-fold.

Read: Ephesians 2:19-22   Ephesians 4:11-13
Romans 8:29-30

The five-fold are called by Christ. They are one with Christ. Their anointing is given to them by Christ. Therefore, their unity is found in Christ.

The mandate for the five-fold is found in Ephesians 4. Therefore, they better be on the same "page" as they build the church up into maturity. That "page" is Christ.

Today, ask the Holy Spirit how to pray for the apostles, prophets, evangelists, pastors and teachers.

NOVEMBER 11

Agreement by the Holy Spirit in love.

Read: 1 Corinthians 1:10-13 1 Corinthians 3:4-9

When we are able to see that Jesus is the focus, we can have agreement with each other in love. For without love, nothing counts as anything, anyway. Therefore, the five-fold should be in agreement with each other by the Holy Spirit in love.

If there is division, it means somewhere one or both parties are not agreeing with the Holy Spirit. The Bride of Christ will not have division and the five-fold will lead the way in this by being in agreement with each other by the Holy Spirit *in love*.

Command the enemy to be quiet and removed from your presence. Then ask the Holy Spirit where you need to agree with Him today.

NOVEMBER 12

Exclusivity of the Five-Fold.

Read: Matthew 22:14   Romans 8:29-30

Cambridge Dictionary Definition of Exclusivity: "The right to have or do something that is limited to only one person or organization."

For those of us who have grown up in a republic or a democracy, exclusivity in the church may rub us the wrong way. But in the Kingdom of God, God gets to choose. Therefore, Jesus chooses His five-fold ministers, and it's not based on merit. This means that one cannot work themselves into a position of evangelist or prophet or any other office. One is either called or not, and that calling is by the Lord Himself.

The rest of the body of Christ also has gifts and callings, and we all work together for the common goal of bringing Heaven to earth.

Today, praise the Lord that He chooses! That He is wise and all-knowing! That His ways are awesome!

Rejecting the gifts to the church?

Read: Romans 6:23   Mark 7:9

Jesus wants to know – *"How is it that men can reject My five-fold gifts to the church, but they think so highly of salvation, which is also My gift to the church?"*

The answer lies in the amount of benefit to each person. People see the personal benefit of salvation. But the gift of the five-fold ministers messes with men's desires and how they think or want something to go.

The Lord asks, *"Do you value one gift more highly than another? Could it be because you don't understand the values I've placed on My gifts?"*

Talk to the Holy Spirit about this today.

The Five-Fold Ministers will be judged more harshly.

Read: James 3:1 NIV Luke 12:48b

The five-fold ministers (apostles, prophets, evangelists, pastors, and teachers) have been entrusted with much. And the Lord says that to whom much is given, more will be demanded.

It's notable that they are not judged on who follows them or the amount of attention they attract, but how well they follow the Holy Spirit. This is why James exhorts people not to presume to be something they are not. It's because the judgment is stricter. However, it is still true that just as the rest of the church, the five-fold ministers are judged on how they follow the Lord.

Today, pray for those in the five-fold to follow the Holy Spirit in all things.

November 15

Those who come in His Name, whom He sends.

Read: Luke 10:16

Can you see why listening to the Holy Spirit is so important when you think of this verse? Have you ever dismissed someone coming in the name of the Lord because you didn't care for their style or what they said? Can you see why it would be important to listen to the Holy Spirit before rejecting someone outright?

The LORD says that you don't discern the things of the Spirit by using the natural. So spiritual fruit is spiritually discerned. Spirit gives birth to spirit. You must look in the Spirit. It's like judging by what you hear, not necessarily what you see. For instance, you may see power, and think the person with power comes in the name of the LORD, but you still need to listen to the Holy Spirit to make an accurate judgment.

Today, ask the Lord for greater discernment to see and hear in the Spirit that you may know what is from Him and what is not.

NOVEMBER 16

His Kingdom is a Kingdom, not a Republic or a Democracy.

Read: Daniel 4:34-37   Revelation 19:16

The Lord is over His Kingdom. He is the King and it's according to His way. It's not dependent on what people want to do or the majority voting on something. Therefore, the Kingdom of God is such that we don't get to decide how it's run. He has decided and our desire is to bring His Kingdom to earth, His way.

When we pray the Lord's Prayer, we are calling for His kingdom to come on earth in the same way that it is in Heaven. Be submitted to His desires, and this will be an exciting prayer for you to pray!

Ask the Holy Spirit to open your eyes today to see the Kingdom of Heaven like never before.

November 17

Father says, "Can you see that I put everything in My Son's hands?"

Read: Colossians 1:13-19

Jesus told us how His church should be – without spot or wrinkle. He's the Head of the Church, and it will be like Jesus wants or it won't be. Father gave the Church to Jesus and it's going to be how Jesus says.

All things have been given into Jesus' hands. He holds all things together, and He is King of kings and Lord of lords. Is there anything for which Christ is not preeminent?

Today, praise the Father for placing all things in Jesus' hands!

The Church has to be according to the Son because of love.

Read: John 17:24   John 15:9   John 3:16

Father says, *"Even as much as I love the people, I love the Son. I have said the church will be under Him. He's the Head. Therefore, the church has to be according to My Son because of love."*

Christ laid down His life for the church. Has anyone loved the church as much as the Son? Because the Son's love is so great for the church, it must be according to Christ.

Ponder the love of the Father for the Son and the Son for the Church today.

November 19

If a church doesn't have life, it doesn't have Me. (Not The Church, but a church.)

Read: John 14:6   John 1:1-4

Jesus is the Way, the Truth, and the Life. So, if there is no life, He is not there. There is no life outside of Him.

And if He is present, you will recognize the Life and the Spirit moving. The Kingdom of Heaven comes when the Spirit moves. So, you will see things like healing and deliverance happening. You will hear prophetic words given. You will receive revelation and understanding.

It will not be dead religion. If there is no life, there is no Jesus.

Command the enemy to be silent and ask the Holy Spirit if there is life where you are attending church. Ask Him to show you proof. Then wait and be still. He will speak to you.

NOVEMBER 20

If a church has no life, then leave.

Read: 1 Peter 2:4-5   2 Corinthians 6:14
       1 Thessalonians 5:5

If you are a living stone, then you are alive. You are part of a living body, whose Head is Christ. Each part is instructed to do its share for the working of the whole body.

If there are dead stones mixed with the living, there is not a healthy body working together according to the direction of the Head. What kind of fellowship can light have with darkness anyway?

You were bought with a price and the light of Christ shines in you. Go where there is life and light. Fellowship with true believers. The Spirit is always moving; living water moves. So, if there is no life, then leave!

NOVEMBER 21

My Spirit is always moving.

Read: John 3:8   John 7:38

Just as water must move or it will become stagnant, so the Spirit of the Lord moves, for He is Life. This means some things will change. Be prepared for it, and don't resist the change that comes from the Holy Spirit.

The Lord says, *"My Spirit is always moving. If you're following the traditions of men only, get out! Those don't move, and you should be able to tell the difference."*

Ask where the Spirit is moving today and move with Him!

NOVEMBER 22

My Church is financed by Me, not by witchcraft.

Read: Luke 12:22-34

Witchcraft is manipulation. It's trying to get something using any means besides the power/Spirit of God. When we try to guilt people to give to our church or ministry by telling them it's part of the law that they have to obey, or telling them they won't be blessed unless they give to us, that is all witchcraft. Those who trust in the Lord, however, will see how He provides for them. They need not worry, for their Father knows what they need and desires to bless them.

You may want to read the testimony of George Mueller sometime. He never asked for money, but he ran several orphanages in England in the 1800's. At one point, he and the orphans sat down to breakfast with nothing to eat or drink. They gave thanks to God for their breakfast and then there was a knock at the door. It was the baker. He had gotten up early and baked many, many loaves of bread for the orphans. He felt God was telling him to. Then he left, and there was another knock at the door. The milkman's cart broke down right in front of the orphanage, and so he was wondering if they wanted the milk for free.

God is not a respecter of persons. What He did for the orphans in Mueller's day, he's still able and willing to do today. He's looking for faith. Faith opposes witchcraft, because witchcraft depends on self and how self can manipulate others.

The true church of God will not use witchcraft, but will operate in faith.

NOVEMBER 23

Apostles and Prophets lay the foundation.

Read: Ephesians 2:19-22   Galatians 1:11-12

Jesus is the Rock, and the apostles and prophets lay the foundation off of that Rock. All revelation is the unveiling of Jesus Christ, so everything the apostles and prophets bring to the church should help to build that firm foundation. They are the ones the Lord has chosen to give His revelation to, so it is of the utmost importance that they have their rightful places in the body of Christ.

Without the apostles and prophets, our foundation will be shaky at best. Prophets bring the word of the Lord, and apostles reveal Him. The prophetic word gives you direction, vision. The apostolic revelation grounds you. Together they form the right foundation for building. Even prophecy is revelatory in nature and so it all lifts up Jesus

Prayer: Father we intercede for the apostles and prophets today. We ask that you fill them with revelation and grant them prophecy. Show them Jesus that they may bring what You say to the body of Christ, and we may all be built up together for a dwelling place of God in the Spirit. Amen.

NOVEMBER 24

Evangelist, Pastors, and Teachers do not have the privilege of generating theology.

Read: Ephesians 3:1-5

As you read through the Scriptures, it becomes evident that revelation (knowledge into the mystery of God) for the church comes through the apostles and prophets. There are some people who wrote Scripture who were not apostles or prophets, like Luke. However, Luke's writing was not revelatory in nature, but an account of the life of Jesus, or we could say an account of the testimony of Jesus. This is different from John, Peter, Paul, James, or Jude's letters. It's even different from the books in the Old Testament written by the prophets.

The evangelists, pastors, and teachers do their part to build up the body of Christ for the work of ministry, but they do not come up with theology. They take what the Lord has revealed to the apostles and prophets, and they bring that to the body of Christ. The roles of each of the five-fold ministers are different, and for good reason. Jesus creates us uniquely to fulfill the roles that He has designed for us to do. When we all do our part, it glorifies the Lord!

NOVEMBER 25

Did Paul actually minister with Jesus? If not, that makes him a different kind of apostle, doesn't it?

Read: Acts 1:15-26   Romans 16:7

We see in Acts 1 that only those who physically were with Jesus while He was here in the flesh were considered to be part of the 12 apostles. And yet, there were other apostles called as well, as we can see from the other Scriptures. Yet, these apostles didn't follow Jesus when He was walking in the flesh on the earth.

Paul was the first of his kind. He was the first of those apostles who did not minister with Jesus in the flesh. Some other apostles mentioned in the Scriptures are Jesus' two brothers, James and Jude, who both mocked Him when He ministered on earth because they did not believe in Him (John 7:3-5). James actually ended up leading the apostles in Jerusalem. Then there's Junia and Adronicus. They were not part of the original 12 apostles either, and yet they were highly esteemed as apostles and served time in prison with Paul. (Romans 16:7)

Jesus gave apostles, prophets, evangelists, pastors and teachers to His church to build her up and equip her for the works of ministry. He continues to do that today. He trains up these leaders by His Spirit in the same way He did for Paul.

NOVEMBER 26

The five-fold ministers lay down their lives to help the saints complete the vision God has for them.

Read: Ephesians 4:11-13 NKJV   1 John 3:16

The five-fold ministers (apostles, prophets, evangelists, pastors & teachers) are called to lay down their lives to equip the saints for the work of ministry. This means that whatever vision God has given to others, the five-fold ministers are helping them achieve that goal.

Jesus is always our example, and Jesus did precisely this. He laid down His life in order that we may come to Father. This is what we see the Apostle Paul did. He suffered so that others could come to Christ and reach the goal God had for them. It's what the Chinese underground church does. It's what the believers in Muslim countries do.

We're all called to lay our lives down for Jesus, but those who are chosen by Christ to be in the five-fold are called to lay down their lives for the saints in order that they may complete the vison God has for them.

Ponder these things with the Holy Spirit as you go about your day today.

NOVEMBER 27

The five-fold ministers are the Jesus way.

Read: Ephesians 4:11-16

Salvation is not the only gift Jesus gave. He also gave the apostles, prophets, evangelists, pastors, and teachers. These are appointed by Him and not by men.

Since Jesus gave the five-fold ministers to the church as a gift. Do we really think we can do it another way? If we follow Jesus, we do it His way. He set up His church. He desires it to be His way. If we follow Him, we, too, will desire it to be His way and not another way.

Jesus is coming back for an unblemished bride. This will not happen without the five-fold ministers in their rightful places, because they are the ones tasked to equip the church for the works of the ministry.

Receive the gifts Jesus gave and thank Him for them, today!

NOVEMBER 28

Jesus is the head of the church.

Read: Colossians 1:18   Ephesians 4:15-16

Can a body function without its head? Of course not. Can a body move without its head? Can it do anything? So then, what directs the body, if not the head?

Therefore, if Jesus is the head of His body – the Church, shouldn't He be the one directing how it goes? We, who have put our trust in Him, make up His body. But He is the One who directs His body, for He is the Head. Therefore, things in the church should go the way that Jesus directs them, the way He sets them up, the way He desires them.

Ask the Holy Spirit to show you Jesus as the Head of His church, today. Write down what He shows you. You may want to look at it another time.

NOVEMBER 29

The Church another way is not the Church. He's the Way. It's His Church.

Read: Colossians 1:15-18 NKJV   Proverbs 14:12 NKJV
Proverbs 16:25 NKJV

If all things have been created through Jesus and for Jesus, why would we try to do church in any other way? Why would we think we could do something for Jesus, but not His way?

This is like going to your job and having your boss tell you how he wants something done. You decide, however, that you don't really want to do it that way, or you think you have a better way. So, you do it how you want. Will your boss be pleased? Hasn't he hired you to do a certain work the way he desires it to be done?

Now, with a human boss, it may be that you actually do have a better way to get the job done. But with Jesus, do you think that's the case? And yet, over the years, man has decided to do "church" his own way, rather than the way of the Lord. Sounds like "the way that seems right to a man."

Why do you think Jesus would set up His church in a way that seems offensive to some people? Command the atmosphere to be clear and ask the Holy Spirit about this.

NOVEMBER 30

How would someone with the Spirit of Christ settle differences with another follower of Jesus Christ?

Read: Philippians 4:2-3   1 Corinthians 1:10
2 Corinthians 13:11

For those of us with the Holy Spirit, we must settle differences by the Holy Spirit. To do this, we must have the same thoughts. But how do we get there when we're divided in what we think or believe?

The answer is always Jesus. Who did Jesus agree with? He always agreed with Father. Father, Son, and Holy Spirit are all of the same opinion. They perfectly agree. In fact, the Lord does not have two opinions on a matter. He only has one. This is why He never budged when He was opposed. He knew He was agreeing with the Holy Spirit. And those who followed Him had to agree with the Holy Spirit, too, even when it flew in the face of what they thought was right.

Therefore, the only way that we can agree with one another in Christ is to agree with Him. This is how you can easily settle any difference between believers. If you decide you always want to agree with the Holy Spirit, this will not be difficult for you. You will have to give up pride, which always wants to be right, but once you decide to do that, it will be easy.

And for those who are filled with the Holy Spirit, this ought to be what they desire. They ought to desire to agree with the Lord. To disagree with Him, is to agree with a lie because truth is in Him alone.

Today, tell Holy Spirit, you are choosing to agree with Him on all things. Then get ready. A difference with another believer will likely come up and you will have an opportunity to agree with God.

December 1

Can unity be accomplished any other way than the Spirit of Christ?

Read: Ephesians 2:14-18

If we're talking about unity, there is only unity in Christ. There is conformity in the world, but in Christ there is unity. The tower of Babel was built because they all had the same agenda. They wanted to reach heaven with their own strength and power. But as soon as the Lord confused their languages, they stopped. There wasn't any unity. It was simply conformity.

In Christ, even language is not a barrier. Galatians 3:27-28 reads, **"For as many of you as were baptized into Christ have put on Christ. There is neither Jew nor Greek, there is neither slave nor free, there is neither male nor female; for you are all one in Christ Jesus."**

In Christ, we are all one because we are all in Christ, and all partake of the same Spirit – the Spirit of Christ. There's really no other way to have true unity than the Spirit of Christ. Without Him, you may have conformity, you may be united around a purpose or an ideal, but you will not have true unity.

It is Jesus who has broken down the wall of separation between us and united us in Himself. Praise God!

DECEMBER 2

There are so many ways that people have believed the Scriptures; is it possible for the Spirit of Christ to reconcile all of these?

Read: Romans 12:9-21   Philippians 4:2-3

In these passages of Scripture, we get an idea of how we are to relate to one another. In particular, we want to focus on the command to "be of the same mind," and relate this to differences of opinion on the meaning of Scripture.

Most of the time, people believe that in order for us all to be of the same mind, we have to conform to something. Maybe we conform to the doctrines of our particular denomination, or we conform to a particular ideology or teacher of the Scriptures.

However, in Christ, there is not conformity. There is unity. That unity, as we've been talking about, only comes by the Holy Spirit. True unity with other believers is found by agreeing with the Holy Spirit. That is also where true humility is found.

Therefore, being of the same mind, means we each agree with the Holy Spirit. What does He say the Scripture means? If you don't hear Him regarding it, then just admit you don't know yet. Until you hear Him on it, allow yourself to be at peace with the other person. He may speak through an apostle on the subject in question, or He may speak to you, directly. But many times, it will come through an apostle or prophet.

So instead of agreeing to disagree, wait for the revelation of the Lord and agree with that. In the meantime, be at peace. Be of the same mind as the Holy Spirit. Amen.

How would your church accommodate a teen with the gift of prophecy?

Read: 1 Thessalonians 5:19-21

The Holy Spirit would like us to <u>accommodate</u> teens with the gift of prophecy in the same way we would accommodate anyone else who has the gift of prophecy. We do this by allowing them to prophesy. When they believe they are hearing something from the Lord, they need to be allowed to speak it. Then the word can be tested by seeking the Holy Spirit regarding what has been said. If there is correction needed, it can be given. If not, commend the teen for sharing what they've heard.

We can also <u>encourage</u> a teen with the gift of prophesy. Instead of waiting for them to speak up, we could actually ask them if they feel the Holy Spirit is saying something regarding whatever is being taught or discussed. In this way, they would be encouraged to listen for a word of prophecy, and so learn better to walk in the gift the Holy Spirit has given them.

Feel free also as you pray in your church to stir up the gift of prophecy; and ask the Holy Spirit to prophesy through those present.

DECEMBER 4

What if a teen in your church is more anointed than the adults? What do you do?

Read: Acts 4:1-4, 13-14

Instead of looking at the age of a person, or their educational background, or criteria the world considers, look at their anointing. The passage we read in Acts is a great example of this. Peter and John were unschooled, ordinary men. They didn't have an education, and they weren't an elder of the people. But their message and the power of the Holy Spirit through them brought about the rebirth of 5,000 men. That's incredible.

Would a teen with a greater anointing than the adults be encouraged to minister in your church? Or, would it be embarrassing to have someone younger and more inexperienced leading things in your church? If it would be embarrassing, you would need to ask why that would be the case. We'll delve more deeply into it tomorrow, but we must first understand that if God anoints someone, who are we to hold them back? And not just that, but shouldn't we encourage them in what God has anointed them to do?

In this, it helps to think of Jesus. Would He be holding a teen back because they were not an adult? Would He make a mistake in anointing a teen more than the adults?

Prayer: Father, give us eyes to see the anointing on others and the grace to encourage them in Jesus' name, amen.

December 5

Is there a spirit of pride in your church?

Read: 1 Samuel 18:5-9

In King Saul, we see a great example of pride. The Scriptures testify that David behaved wisely, or prospered, everywhere Saul sent him. In other words, he excelled at everything he was sent to do; so much so that the women sang songs about him. Instead of commending David, Saul became jealous and angry.

A good leader encourages someone like David and rejoices at the anointing of the Lord on his life. Unfortunately, pride holds others back when they should be encouraged.

Is this how your church operates? Is there a spirit of pride that holds others back, so they don't "one up" the leadership? How can you make your ceiling, the floor of the next generation if you don't encourage them to go past where you are?

Jesus laid down His life so that we could be exalted to a position of sonship. If we're following Him, that will be our attitude, too.

DECEMBER 6

Does your church exist to make the congregants look good, or to lift Jesus ever higher?

Read: Acts 5:1-11

Had Ananias and Sapphira been allowed to continue in their deceit, would Jesus have been lifted higher? Who would have looked good? Ananias and Sapphira, right?

Peter's act of calling them out and pronouncing judgment on them put a stop to doing things to make the congregants look good. The Bible records that fear came upon the church and all who heard of it.

When we do things for the purpose of making the congregants look good, we are exalting ourselves, and not Jesus. He is the Head of His church. He is our love, our life, and the purpose for which we exist.

Therefore, check the heart motives behind the activities your church is involved in. This can only be done by listening to the Holy Spirit. And before you ask the Holy Spirit, use your authority to silence the voice of the enemy, so you're not just hearing criticism.

DECEMBER 7

If a teen was known to be a member of the five-fold, how would your church train him or her?

Read: Ephesians 4:11-12

These two verses in Ephesians give a big picture overview of the five-fold ministry. These apostles, prophets, evangelists, pastors, and teachers are given to the church to equip the body of Christ to minister in the Spirit of Christ – to bring the gospel to the world. In order for teens to mature, they need to practice their office.

Let's look at this in the context of a house church. There may be a pastor who is leading a house church, and that house church is under an apostle and prophet who may oversee several house churches in the area. That pastor knows that there is a teen who has been chosen by Jesus to be an apostle. That pastor may ask the teen to seek the Lord for direction on how to direct the next meeting. The teen would go home, speak to Holy Spirit, and get a vision for how to direct next week's meeting. They would come back and be allowed to "be in charge" of that meeting. If there was correction needed, it would gently be given, for all desire this teen to excel in his or her calling.

Using this example of a teen called as an apostle, it may be that the church would gather around that teen at some point and ask the Holy Spirit to bring a prophet to help this apostolic teen in their ministry. They may lay hands on the teen apostle and prophesy over him or her. They may ask for another apostle to come and help to instruct the teen in the ways of an apostle.

There are many ways to help a teen who is known to be part of the five-fold. If we understand these five-fold ministers are gifts to the church, then we are going to want them to mature in all ways. That requires us to help them any way we can; so that they can do their job well and help the rest of the church. Their age should not even be a factor to us in this.

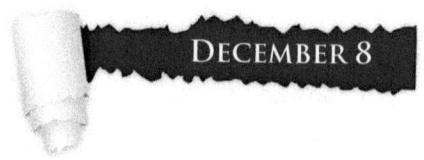

How does your church raise up teens in the gifts of the Spirit?

Read: 1 Corinthians 12:1 & 14:1

The Bible is pretty clear that we are to understand the gifts of the Spirit and that we are to pursue the spiritual gifts. There's no age limitations put on that knowledge and pursuit. That means the teens in your church should be encouraged to pursue the gifts of the Spirit and be taught what they are and how they operate.

So, look around you and see what your church is doing in this regard. Do they actively raise up teens in the gifts of the Spirit? Does your church operate in the gifts, or even understand them? It's hard to raise up teens to do what the adults, themselves, are not doing.

It's very important that the teens are operating in the gifts of the Spirit. If we're disciples of Jesus, bringing the message of the gospel of the Kingdom to the world, we can't do it without power, and that power is poured out in the gifts of the Spirit of God.

Command the enemy to be silent and then speak to the Holy Spirit about these things today.

December 9

Teenagers separate from church because they're held separate from the church.

Read: 1 Corinthians 12:12-22

When we separate teens from us, we're basically saying, "We don't need you." Is it any wonder then that the teens leave?

In the home church setting, teens are not separate. This is ideal. In the institutional church, they are separated most of the time. Leadership in these churches have tried many things to keep the teens in their churches. They try programs, games, activities, food, competitions, and other entertainment of all sorts to try and keep the teens from leaving their churches. But the Lord says that the teens leave the church because they're left out. What they're being fed is not even milk all the time, but mostly nonsense.

Look again at the Scripture reading for today. The body of Christ has many parts, and each part is necessary. When we separate the teens from the body, what does that mean for them and for the rest of the body? What happens if you take off one of your legs, or your eyes, or your ears? The part that you removed dies off because it's separate, and the rest of the body doesn't function at full capacity anymore.

This is serious to the Lord. He doesn't want His body separate, but whole. One body. You'll find the teens staying united with the rest of the body of Christ when you don't try to separate them.

DECEMBER 10

"My Church is one."

Read: Ephesians 4:4   Galatians 3:27-28

When Jesus looks at His body – the Church – He doesn't see a bunch of different groups. He sees one body moving together by the Spirit of the Lord.

This means, the body is not a bunch of different denominations, it's not men's groups or women's groups, it's not teen groups or children's groups. It's not divided up into what you think you're good at or what your interests are. Jesus says that there are not men's issues or women's issues or children's issues; there are spiritual issues. The body of Christ is one. So, instead of dividing His body up into different groups, see His body as one, moving as one, and operating as one.

This oneness is only achieved by the Spirit of the Lord. When you are of the Spirit, you can recognize others who are of the Spirit. The Body is of One Spirit and One Lord. This is how Jesus sees it and so this is how it is.

CHILDREN

Should children be exposed to things like prophecy? Healing? Other power gifts of the Holy Spirit?

Read: Romans 8:9-11   John 3:34

These verses from Romans, among others, tell us that we have received the same Spirit that raised Christ from the dead, meaning His Spirit – the Holy Spirit. This is the Spirit of Prophecy, Healing, and all the other gifts of the Spirit. When we receive the Holy Spirit, we receive the same Spirit as Christ.

And the verse in John tells us that Father gives the Spirit without measure, meaning He doesn't give Him just a little bit for some and more for others.

But, what about children? Do they receive that same Spirit? Is there a junior Holy Spirit? Does the Holy Spirit only come on children in part until they're older? Is God afraid to pour out His Spirit on a child in fear that they won't be able to handle what He says to them or does through them? Does the Holy Spirit hold back on some of His gifts when it comes to children, reserving them only for adults?

There is no distinction between children and adults regarding the outpouring of the Holy Spirit. He is for everyone who believes and desires to carry Him, including children. And He comes with gifts! That means children can prophesy, pray in tongues, heal, give words of wisdom and knowledge, and operate in whatever other gift the Holy Spirit gives them.

Therefore, children need to be exposed to prophecy, healing, and other power gifts of the Holy Spirit. The Holy Spirit, remember, is the Comforter. That's not just so He can comfort us when we're downcast, but also because some things He does may be uncomfortable for us.

So, allow the children to come to Jesus and don't deny them access to His Spirit and what His Spirit desires to do.

December 12

Is it a parent's decision when their child should experience baptism, gifts of the Spirit, etc.? Or is it God's decision?

Read: Matthew 19:13-15   Matthew 18:6

For this question, we really need to consider who is in control of our children's lives. Is it us? Or is it God? Has He created children for Himself or for us? Do we really desire God to have His way in our children's lives, or do we want things to go our way for our children? Do we know better than God?

We may think we've given our children over to God and that we desire His will to be done in their lives. But what if someone lays hands on your child and they receive the Holy Spirit, speaking in tongues and prophesying? Will you be offended if you weren't there? What if your child is somewhere without you and desires to be baptized in water? Will you be upset if they are baptized outside of your presence? Or, maybe they desire some gift of the Spirit and you tell them to wait for some reason.

Are you Lord, or is Jesus? Is their walk with Christ about you, or about Him and He in them?

It is obvious from what Jesus has said that if we stand in the way of our children coming to Him in any way, we become a stumbling block to our children. We cannot do that.

Today, speak to the Holy Spirit about these things, and if necessary, release your children to the LORD, holding nothing back.

DECEMBER 13

Why would parents be upset if their child has an experience with the Lord (think baptism, born again, gifts of the Spirit, prophecy, etc.)?

Read: 1 John 5:21   Colossians 3:5 (NIV)   Luke 9:23

For today's devotional, the Holy Spirit is going a little further than yesterday's devotional. He says that there are believing parents who become offended, angry, upset, even sad, if their child has a spiritual experience without them being present or without them instigating the experience.

This is rooted in selfishness. If we are determining for our children what their experience with God will be, and when it will happen, and that it can't happen without us, then we are exalting ourselves to the head position in their lives. There is One head of the church, and He is Christ.

Self always wants to be pre-eminent in all things; and will even use Scripture and logic to justify its behavior; but God is not fooled. Either Jesus is Lord, or He isn't. He tells us to deny ourselves – what we think, what we want, how we think things should go – and follow Him (His way, His thoughts, how He wants it to go).

Therefore, put on love, which never fails. Your child's life isn't about you. It's about Jesus. Pray for your children, speak life over them, declare over them the things God has to say about them. And don't get in the way of what the Holy Spirit desires to do. Trust Him. He has your child's best interests at heart. He can ONLY do good. So praise Him for every experience your child has with Him!

December 14

How should we make decisions in parenting? By logic??

Read: Proverbs 14:12   Jeremiah 6:16

"**There is a way that seems right to a man, But its end is the way of death.**" In other words, sometimes a way seems like it would be good to us, but it's the wrong way, or the wrong choice. We cannot depend on our intellect or logic to decide things. The way that we should make decisions is to stop, look, ask, and ask.

Wisdom is found in Christ because He has become for us wisdom from God (1 Corinthians 1:30). What we think will never lead to wisdom. It's what He says that is wisdom. This is why when we need to make a decision regarding our children, we stop, look in the spirit at what Father is doing, ask the Holy Spirit what to do, and ask again to make sure we got it right. Then do what He says. Believe Him.

Is your child struggling in school? Do you need help disciplining? How about what activities your children should be in? How much electronic time? What kind of electronics? What about your children's eating habits? What about medical advice? The questions are endless, but the answer is to stop and look and ask and ask. Do not lean on your own understanding. Seek Him! He knows what's best and He wants what's best.

DECEMBER 15

Could you take a word from the Lord if it came through a child?

Read: 1 Samuel 3 (especially verses 16-18)

Samuel was a young child when he first received a word from the Lord. Eli was an elderly man at the time and despite his experience and authority, he was willing to receive what Samuel had to say. He recognized the voice of the Holy Spirit in what Samuel was saying.

When we walk with the Lord, we, too, will recognize His voice in what others say. So, even if the word of the Lord comes through a child who lacks maturity, we will be able to recognize it is the Lord.

Remember that God uses the foolish to shame the wise and the weak to shame the strong and those that are nothing to shame those who are. (1 Corinthians 1:27-28) So, do not dismiss what a child is saying, simply because they are young. Listen for the voice of the Holy Spirit, regardless of who is speaking.

DECEMBER 16

Is it possible for parents to be in unity in raising children?

Read: Luke 1:5-17

Is it possible for parents to be in unity in raising children? Absolutely. But in order to be in unity at all times, you need to both be committed to following and desiring what God wants for your child, over what you want. Remember that you're not desiring your children to be conformed into your image, but into the image of Christ. If this is true for both parents, you can definitely raise your children in unity.

Zacharias and Elizabeth were given instructions from the Lord on how to raise John. They were also given a prophetic word for his life – what John's call was and his destiny. They used those words to raise him, even before the Spirit was poured out. If two people can use just a few words from the Lord to raise their son in unity, certainly we, who have the Holy Spirit and talk to Him daily, can raise our children in unity together.

So, as you raise your children, seek the Lord in the big and little things. Believe He speaks to you and that you hear Him. Then follow Him.

DECEMBER 17

It's not about filtering out the bad; it's about freely releasing the good.

Read: Proverbs 22:6

When you train children in the way that they should go, you are training them to follow the Holy Spirit. You are showing them the good way, the good path, how to make good choices. Instead of focusing on stopping the bad in every situation, you are focusing on showing them how to choose the good.

You can't stop every bad thing, but if you freely release good, your kids will know the difference between good and bad and learn to choose good.

Therefore, focus on showing them the right way. Do not be discouraged if they do not always make the right choices or they become deceived in some area. Take the word of the Lord to heart that He has promised if you train your child in the way they should go – the way of the Spirit- when they are old, they will not depart from it. They will choose Him.

Believe God and show your kids the good way. He will not forsake you in this. The way of the Spirit is the right way. Model it by doing it yourself, and train them by showing them how to listen and obey as well.

What does godly discipline look like?

Read: Proverbs 13:24   Hebrews 12:7-11

Some have taken the verse in Proverbs as an excuse to beat their children. That is obviously not godly discipline. These two Scripture passages from Hebrews and Proverbs are telling us that discipline is necessary in order to train a child. God, Himself, disciplines us, or corrects us. If we are like Him, we, too, will discipline and correct our children.

Each child is different, however, and it may be necessary to alter discipline tactics for each child. One child may need electronics taken away for a while. Another child may need something else. In each case, you will need listen to the Holy Spirit to determine what would work best in each situation for each child. Jesus knows your children better than you do. He created them!

You will also need to make sure you are disciplining in love. If you feel the enemy is bringing you into a place of pride or anger as you discipline, you need to stop yourself. Back away and listen. Then come back and bring the discipline when you know you are doing it in love. Love never fails, and if you discipline in love – which you can only do by following the Spirit, it will not fail to bring about "the peaceable fruit of righteousness" in your children.

And remember, the goal is to help your children to follow the Holy Spirit. Keep the goal in mind and always operate in love.

DECEMBER 19

Is it a benefit to know your child's destiny? Should you seek God on this? Perhaps ask a prophet?

Read: John 16:13   Matthew 7:7-8

Proverbs 29:18 (KJV) states, "**Where there is no vision, the people perish: but he that keepeth the law, happy is he.**" In the Old Covenant, the law was the vision the people kept because it was the vision of the right way. In the New Covenant, we follow the Holy Spirit. The law of the Spirit is the vision we keep in front of us because the Spirit shows us the right way, not the written law. For each of us, the right way, or the right path, will be different. We will each be doing what is right morally by following the Holy Spirit. When we have a vision from Him, we will be following the right path to our destiny.

Having a vision for your child will also help you to see in them what God sees in them and to fight the battles that come with the Sword of the Spirit – the Word of the Lord – that has been given to you regarding your child. One of the things Holy Spirit does is He tells us things to come. He is the Spirit of Prophecy. So, He prophesies, and that includes prophesying about your child's future. Therefore, if you don't know your child's future, ask. Jesus says if we ask, we shall receive. He may speak to you, He may speak to your child, He may speak through a prophet or someone else. But He will tell you. He wants to!

Prayer: Holy Spirit, please show us the destinies of our children. We desire to know. We desire to call it forth and pray it forth. We desire to see in our children what you see in them. Thank You! Amen.

December 20

Is there ever a time when a parent should stand in the way of something that the Holy Spirit wants to do for their child?

Read: Ephesians 4:4-6

There is One Lord, and it's not you. If the Holy Spirit wants to do something in your child's life, and you stand in the way of it, you have elevated what you think is right above what the Lord thinks is right. If you are elevating your thoughts above the Lord's, you've made yourself the higher one in the relationship between you and God.

Your child is under your authority. But that authority is not given to you so that you can be an authoritarian. It's given to you so that you can help your child learn to follow the Holy Spirit, so that you can train them up in the way that they should go. God knows the way they should go, and if you are listening to Him, you will be able to assist your child in following Him.

Remember that children are created for Him. Be willing to allow Him to do what He desires in your child's life, even if you don't understand or you don't think it's quite right. Trust Him. He really loves your child even more than you do. Remember that He gave His Son for your child. How will He not along with Him, graciously give us all things? (Romans 8:32)

DECEMBER 21

What should a parent expect or look for in a church for their children? Should the children participate in the same way as the adults?

Read: Luke 9:10-11, 37-38   1 Corinthians 16:19   Philemon 1:2

When Jesus taught, there were entire families there. When the apostles set up house churches in cities, they met in houses – homes where there would be children.

We've discussed previously how there is no junior Holy Spirit. So, the Holy Spirit the adults receive, is the same One the children receive. Therefore, the Holy Spirit can bring understanding to a child just as He can an adult. He speaks to us how we understand, and we *can* understand, despite age differences.

Additionally, His power is for all of us. Faith is not based on age. If anything, children tend to have more faith than adults.

A lot of times when parents are looking for a church to attend, they look for programs for their children to be involved in. They try to determine how much emphasis is placed on the kids' programs, clubs, classes, etc. We've been indoctrinated with the thought that children need to have their own church, while the adults have theirs. But the Lord is saying this isn't so. We need to be open and honest in our churches and allow the children to be trained up like the adults. In an institutional church, this will be difficult, if not impossible. But in a house church setting, this is natural, and works well.

Don't worry about whether or not your child can handle it. Allow the Holy Spirit to determine what your child can handle.

DECEMBER 22

Why is it common to teach children to be bystanders and not participants in church?

Read: Matthew 10:37-38   Matthew 16:24-25

In the institutional church, we've become bystanders, and we've fallen for a lie that seeks to entertain our children, rather than training them in discipleship. We haven't taught them to evangelize, to heal, to deliver, to take authority, to lay down their lives. Instead, we've taught them to be "safe," and stay away from hardship and danger and the need for great faith. And this is because in great part, we don't do any of those things ourselves. We've come to a place where we think this one guy we call "pastor" is supposed to do everything. We pay him to do it. We attend a building once a week with other people who are like-minded, and we think that's Christianity.

It's not so. It's a big lie. Most people who call themselves "Christians" don't really understand what it means to be born again, to be a real disciple. Jesus didn't call people to come to a church building once a week and pay someone to preach to them and offer programs to entertain their children. He called people to lay down their lives and follow Him. He called them to be filled with His Spirit so they could be made like Him and do the things He did and more.

If we are bystanders, can we expect anything more out of our children? Therefore, it starts with us. Determine not to be a bystander. Determine to be a disciple and start following in lock step with your Master. As you do, train your children to do likewise.

Jesus says, *"This is My church. This is the church without spot or wrinkle. This is allowing the little ones to come to Me, and it's not so they can sit on My lap."*

If you are not allowed to <u>not</u> be a bystander in your church, you need to leave. Amen.

DECEMBER 23

Do children's dreams, visions, and words have the same worth as adult's?

Read: Numbers 22:22-35   2 Peter 2:16

When a word is from the Lord, does it matter who it comes through? In our Scripture reading, the donkey's mouth was opened to restrain the prophet's madness. If God can speak through a donkey, He can speak through anyone.

So, the answer to today's question is, yes! Children's dreams, visions, and words have the same worth as an adult's when they come from the Holy Spirit.

What matters when we hear a vision, a dream, or a word is the spirit behind it. Is it from the Holy Spirit or not? That's what matters.

December 24

Should parents pursue interpretation of their children's dreams, visions, words, etc?

Read: Matthew 1:18-25   Matthew 2:13-14

The Lord speaks in many ways. Dreams and visions are just two ways He speaks. If we know that God speaks through dreams, visions, and words – whether they come through adults, children, or even donkeys – then we need to take them seriously. A word from the Lord is serious, regardless of who it comes through, as we learned yesterday.

Additionally, angels are many times involved in the bringing of dreams, visions and words, as well as their interpretations. Sometimes the angels have to battle to get us those dreams, visions, and words. Do we really want to treat it as nothing? If it was important enough for an angel to do battle to get it to us or our child, then it ought to be important enough for us to pursue the interpretation of it.

Therefore, when your child tells you about dreams or visions they have had, go ahead and ask the Holy Spirit together what it means. Your first question to the Lord would be, "Is this dream or vision from You or not?"

If you hear that it is from the Lord, and you are not receiving interpretation, you may want to ask someone else who hears God well. Some people are very gifted at interpretation and it's okay to ask someone else. No one in the body of Christ can do everything all the time by themselves. We need each other.

And always remember that Jesus said if we ask, we will receive; and if we knock, the door will be opened; and if we seek, we will find. So, ask, seek and knock until the answer comes.

December 25

What do parents do if their child is having nightmares or seeing the demonic?

Read: Psalm 91 (NIV)

Yesterday, we discussed how it is important to pursue interpretation for your child's dreams or visions because if God is speaking to them, they need to know what He is saying.

When we ask the Lord, if the dream or vision is from Him, we need to clear the atmosphere first. So, command the enemy to leave your presence and be mute. Then ask the Holy Spirit if the dream or vision is from Him.

Most of the time, if the dream or vision is scary and there seems to be no hope, it is not from the Lord. So, if your child is experiencing nightmares or seeing the demonic, you need to take authority over it and command it to stop.

You may say something like, "I command the atmosphere here clear in Jesus' name! Enemy, get out! I break off these nightmares and demonic visions now in Jesus' name! I speak the blood of Jesus over this room and this child. Holy Spirit, come! Fill this place with your glory." Then call on the angels to come and watch over your child and keep the demonic away from them.

Don't be afraid to do this as often as necessary, but do it in faith, not in fear. You are the one with authority. Use it. (And encourage your child to use their authority to do the same thing.)

December 26

How do parents handle fear in a child?

Read: 2 Timothy 1:7   1 John 4:4   Philippians 2:9-11

There are many verses in the Scriptures that deal with fear. But what the Lord wants us to know today is that handling fear in a child requires listening to the Holy Spirit, just like handling any other issue your child may face.

Fear is a spirit and can be cast out just like any other spirit in the name of Jesus. However, there are times when simply casting out a spirit of fear will not be a long-term fix; because the child has to look at whatever is causing the fear in a different light. In these cases, a child needs to know the truth because it is the truth that sets us free. Reminding a child that Jesus in them is greater than the devil is truth. Letting them know that they do not have to give in to fear just because they "feel" it, will also help. So often, we believe that because we feel something, then it must be true. That is false. We live by faith, and not by sight, or not by our physical senses.

That being said, you will still have to listen to the Holy Spirit because He will give you wisdom in each situation. He will tell you if you simply need to command fear out of the room, or if you need to speak truth to your child, or if you need to do something else.

Whatever He tells you to do, believe it will work because as James testifies: **"Resist the devil, and he will flee from you."** Your resistance is found in whatever the Holy Spirit gives you to do in that moment.

December 27

How do parents decide what's appropriate for a teenager?

Read: 1 Peter 3:10-12   Colossians 3:9

The Lord says the answer for this question is found in honesty. As a parent, are you honest with your teen? Do you explain to them the reasoning for why you do what you do? Do you explain honestly to them how you choose what is appropriate for them?

If you don't feel you can be completely honest with them about your choices for yourself or for them, then you need to ask the Holy Spirit why. You need to be honest with God and with yourself about your choices for yourself and for your teen.

The Lord is saying that teens (and children for that matter) watch what we do, and not just what we say. They know that if you're telling them something is not appropriate for them to do, but you do it, something's amiss. They will see you as a hypocrite and not really believe you. The Lord is saying that honesty will pave the way for righteousness.

The Holy Spirit will tell you what is appropriate for your teen and why. And when He does, be willing to honestly explain to your teen what the Holy Spirit is saying and why. And be willing to change your behavior, if necessary. Honestly come before the Lord and give up what you think is right or what you desire in order to follow Him.

As you do, choosing what is appropriate for your teen based on what you hear from the Holy Spirit will be much easier, and you'll find your teen resisting you a lot less.

December 28

How should parents handle video games?

Read: Deuteronomy 30:19   Philippians 4:8-9

By now, you know that in all decisions, the answer is to ask the Holy Spirit. But as a help to you, the Lord wants to make clear that He is interested in life. In fact, Jesus is Life. So, whatever is Life is good. This is why the verses in Philippians tell us to meditate on good things. Every good and perfect gift is from above, so meditating on the good, turns the thoughts of our hearts to the One who is above all.

The enemy comes to steal, kill, and destroy. Whatever is based in that, is bad. Therefore, what you're allowing in video games, you can look at as either life or death. Sometimes there may be death in a video game, and the Holy Spirit says it's okay. But you should know the content and the spirit behind the game.

Do you know the content of the video games? Is there blood and gore? Is there nudity? Is there witchcraft? You might be surprised just what is in these games.

Choosing life or death would include not just the content of the video games, but how much time is allowed in playing them. Is there any real benefit to playing video games? Sometimes entertainment is fine. The Lord isn't upset with good entertainment, but how much is too much? For this, you need to ask the Holy Spirit and then you need to follow through with what He instructs you.

And with video games, be honest and open about what you expect. Tell your teen you expect them to make good choices. No matter how much you do your homework on a particular game, or how many limits you set, your teen needs to know that they are expected to walk in integrity. This means if they see naked women in their games, or witchcraft going on, they need to turn it off and tell you. If there's swearing, they need to turn it off. (There are ways to shut off the bad language.) If you're gone for the day and they are home, they need to understand that you trust them to be honest with the amount of time they're playing, and that you are trusting them to follow the Holy Spirit and do what is right.

Cultivate honesty and integrity now in your teen's life. Cultivate a relationship of you following and you teaching them to follow the Holy Spirit. Be willing to trust your teen; and be willing to discipline if they go outside the boundaries you've set for them. But then be willing to trust again. Keep this up. When they know they can be trusted and that you and God are for them and not against them, they will desire to do what is right and they will start making good choices.

How should parents handle their teens' bad friends?

Read: 1 Corinthians 15:33 (NIV)   Proverbs 14:7, 22 (NIV)
Proverbs 6:27-28 (NIV)

In these verses, we see that being friends with the wrong people leads us astray. That is pretty obvious.

But your teen may have good intentions of helping the wayward kids at school or befriending those with no friends, even though the reason they have no friends is because they lie, steal or cheat. In all things, we look at Jesus. Who were His friends? Those closest to Him were those who desired the truth. But what do you do if your teen keeps hanging around the wrong crowd?

Your teen's friends don't have to be perfect, but those who are close to your teen should desire what is right and good. They should be trustworthy. There can be those on the outside who your teen talks with and ministers to, but the close friends should be those who are following Jesus, or at the very least, desiring to.

You have authority in your teen's life to help them make good choices. If they are making poor friend choices, you do them a disservice by allowing close friendships with ungodliness.

Therefore, be willing to explain to your teen what God has to say about bad company corrupting good character. Be willing to bring in any testimony from your life that may help them understand how choosing good friends is important. We help those in need, but our friends should be those who follow the Holy Spirit. This cannot be underestimated, and if your teen learns it now, it will save them a lot of grief, later in life, especially as they choose spouses, business partners, etc. And as always, model what you say. Make sure your friends are good friends, too.

Prayer: Jesus, give us wisdom as we deal with bad friends in our teen's lives. Holy Spirit go before us and prepare our teens to see the truth as we speak with them. Fill our mouths with love and wisdom that cannot be refuted in the name of Jesus. And Lord, our teens will follow You! Amen.

DECEMBER 30

Should teens be separated from adults in church, teaching settings, other gatherings?

Read: 1 Corinthians 14:26

Is what you're doing in church different from what your teen is doing? Why would it be? If we are operating as the body of Christ, then when we meet together, we should be building one another up. There should be the sharing of revelation, there may be teaching, there will be songs of praise, prayers of thanksgiving, healing and miracles, tongues and interpretations, prophecy, and more!

Is there anywhere in Scripture where the Holy Spirit makes separate what should happen for teens as opposed to adults when we gather as believers?

If we are truly training our children up in the way they should go, then they need to be with us so that they can learn the right way. They need to be seeing what the Holy Spirit is doing and they need to be operating in the power of the Holy Spirit. How can they be sent out to do what God wants them to do if they are babied all the time? If they never see how it should work in the setting of believers? If they think there's a difference between how God will operate through an adult as opposed to them?

They need to understand that when they are filled with the Holy Spirit, they have the same Spirit as you and Jesus. They need to learn to walk in the fullness of the Spirit and they need whatever revelation and teaching is being brought to the rest of the church.

Therefore, instead of looking for entertainment or a watered-down version of what you do in church, bring your teens in with you and help to train them up in following the Holy Spirit!

DECEMBER 31

How do you raise your child to know good from evil and follow the good when they're teens?

Read: Hebrews 5:11-14 (NIV)

From our reading, we can see that there is training involved in distinguishing good from evil. That training comes with the teaching of righteousness, or the teaching of what is right. As we are taught the right way – the way of the Spirit – we then begin to walk in that way.

The NKJV says that solid food belongs to those who **"by reason of use have their senses exercised to discern both good and evil."** In other words, we use those spiritual senses given to us by the Holy Spirit to discern right and wrong. The teaching in righteousness we receive is then applied to everything. We exercise our senses to discern both good and evil based on the teaching of righteousness.

Look at Jesus. He never did anything He didn't see Father doing and He never spoke anything He didn't hear Father saying. He strictly followed the Holy Spirit in everything. This doesn't mean He wasn't tempted. He definitely was. But He was able to take what Holy Spirit told Him and what He was shown in the Spirit and apply that to discern good from evil.

This is how it works for teens, as well. You help them by teaching them the way of righteousness – showing them how to listen to the

Holy Spirit and obey Him. Encourage them when they are faced with problems and decisions to listen to the Lord and do what they hear. In this way, they will begin to train themselves to distinguish good from evil. They will not just go along with the crowd, and when faced with temptations, they'll actually fight back and overcome.

Prayer: Father, mature our teens so that they will be partakers of the solid food, meant for the mature, and not just milk. Help them to use their senses constantly to distinguish between good and evil by the power of Your Spirit, in the name of Your Son. Amen.

JOURNAL

This area is meant for notetaking and journaling. You may want to write the date of the devotional and/or the topic next to the notes you take on these pages so that you can refer back to the devotional when you need to.

We hope you've been discipled by the Holy Spirit as you've gone through this devotional. We pray that your passion for Jesus grows ever stronger day by day and that you are blessed with the revelation of His great love for you. God bless you!

_____

_____

_____

_____

_____

_____

_____

_____

_____

_____

INDEX

Hearing God
The Lord says, "I have wanted a relationship with each of you since before time began."
God has known you for all time, and yet He desires to speak with you!
How do you start a listening prayer?
Will you give up your own thoughts to hear My voice?
The still small voice.
Come and council with Me you who desire justice; present your case.
My words come with the power to perform themselves.
Speak with Me and I will show you real peace.
Whatever the Holy Spirit hears from Jesus, He speaks to you.
My sheep hear My voice.
My sheep will not follow another.
I speak to you by My Spirit.
I Am the Word; I will not withhold My voice from you.
I AM the Word; I will NOT be silent.
I Am the word; I Am not a book.
Heaven and earth will pass away, but My words will by no means pass away.
Matthew 24:35
Jesus is the Rock.
How did Jesus follow My Spirit?
How did Jesus teach, heal, and deliver?
Who does the talking when you pray?
Give your mind over to Me! Die!
Does your mind wander?
Learn to listen to My voice when you're under pressure.
Settling disagreements requires hearing God, but isn't that mainly for prophets?
How do regular people follow what the Lord is saying?
When should children begin to hear God?

Knowing God
I want people to know Me, not just about Me. I want people to know Me.
Knowing Me is Joy. You can't have the Joy of the LORD and not know Me.
To KNOW Me is to love Me.
My Spirit loves you so much. He's gentle and He wants to know you.
Come to Me boldly. I will never turn you away.
What is truth?

Truth supersedes the facts.
The reality is Christ.
We live and move and have our being because He is Life.
Die continually, or live forever?
No one has seen the Father.
I Am your peace.
I Am the Good Shepherd.
I Am always for you.
I Am never against you.
I Am never the accuser.
No one can come to the Father, except by Me.
I and the Father are One.
Wherever I Am, there is Light.
I Am the LORD.
I do NOT grow weary.
I do not change.
I Am the great <u>I AM</u>!
James 2:19 You believe that there is one God. Good! Even the demons believe that – and shudder!
Theology is Jesus
Could you hear God's voice if He was offending your theology?
Why is Jesus considered our Healer, and we don't really consider Jehovah Rapha?
Did Jesus do the healing, or was it the Spirit working through Him?
What part did the Father play in Jesus' ministry?
What is the difference between knowing God and knowing about Him?
Should we study Judaism since Jesus railed against the Pharisees and the Law?

<u>Baptism</u>

Seeing the Kingdom.
Entering the Kingdom.
How can you know you're saved?
Can you be saved and not have the Holy Spirit?
If you're baptized in the Holy Spirit, do you always have the gift of tongues?
Can you prophesy if you're filled with the Holy Spirit?
Why is the Holy Spirit called "the Spirit of Christ" in the Scriptures?
Have you been baptized in the Holy Spirit?
Continue to press in regarding the baptism of Jesus, My Son. My Spirit will lead you into all Truth.

Baptism of the Holy Spirit.
Fire fall!
Burn Hot!
Why would you want the baptism of the Holy Spirit?
What does it do for a person to have the baptism of the Holy Spirit?
When should children be baptized?

Holy Spirit
Watch for My Spirit to move today.
"Blessed shall you be when you come in, and blessed shall you be when you go out."
Yield to the wind of the Spirit.
The Wind of the Spirit always leads to...?
Jesus is My exact representation.
Jesus has sent you the Promised Holy Spirit.
The Holy Spirit and power.
The Holy Spirit is the Spirit of Christ.
Why is it better that Jesus left?
What does it mean to blaspheme the Holy Spirit?
Shoes come with tongues. So does the Holy Spirit.
What does it mean to blaspheme the Holy Spirit?
What does "the manifest presence" of the Holy Spirit mean?
Why do we picture the Holy Spirit as a dove?
What does the down payment of the Holy Spirit mean?
Does the Holy Spirit promote Himself?
The Holy Spirit speaks what He hears.
Why does it seem like the Holy Spirit is so protected by God?
When God does something, is it always through the Holy Spirit?
What does it mean that the Holy Spirit is our Parakleet (Helper)?
Can you be holy without the Holy Spirit?
Can you be holy as He is holy?
Following the Spirit will agree with Scripture.
Will the Holy Spirit always avoid sharp words?

Gifts of the Holy Spirit
Expect, and by faith receive, gifts from the Holy Spirit, who loves you!
Gifts of the Holy Spirit – the Word of Knowledge.
Gifts of the Holy Spirit – the Word of Wisdom.

Gifts of the Holy Spirit – the Gift of Prophecy.
Gifts of the Holy Spirit – the Gift of Faith.
Gifts of the Holy Spirit – Gifts of Healings.
Gifts of the Holy Spirit – Different kinds of tongues.
Gifts of the Holy Spirit – Interpretation of tongues.
Gifts of the Holy Spirit – Working of Miracles.
Gifts of the Holy Spirit – Discerning of spirits.
Pursuit of the Gifts of the Holy Spirit.
Can you have more than one gift?
If you don't have a particular gift, are you off the hook?
Operating in the Gifts of the Spirit, as Jesus did.
Jesus didn't do what He thought to do.
Why would the Spirit give gifts to men?
Do you need to hold the office of Evangelist to evangelize?
Every disciple will evangelize.
What is the message of Evangelism?
Power Evangelism
The Holy Spirit uses His gifts to evangelize.
Do you think you have to be a Prophet?

In Christ
Can a good tree bring forth bad fruit?
What is the fruit of the Spirit?
What about joy? Whose joy is your strength? Your joy, or God's joy?
What is the purpose of life?
A journey. Will you walk with Me?
Opinions.
What is the reward for bearing good fruit?
What does perfect peace look like?
There's one way. It's the Jesus way.
Strive to enter through the narrow gate.
Look up! For your redemption is near!
Be still.
Come to Me all you who are weary and heavy laden.
I Am your sabbath rest.
I want your burden.
I became sin for you. I will never accuse you of sin.
Without God, you're like a kid at a carnival/amusement park – looking for the next best rollercoaster or fun time.

How do we know how to view ourselves?
What is holiness?
How or why was Jesus holy?
Why did Jesus call Himself the Son of Man?
Can we be considered sons?
Would Jesus be considered our elder brother?
What does it mean to be conformed into the likeness of Christ?
Why is Jesus a Stone of stumbling?
Jesus became sin for us.
What were we given at the death and resurrection of Jesus if we believe?
If you're in Christ, will your life be smooth sailing?
A vision, seeing through My eyes.
An open vision – I want you to come with Me.
If I can't get your attention, will you dream with Me?
Why is vision important?
Do you have a vision for your future?
You will reach the goal through love.

Wisdom & Revelation

Those who have ears, let them hear.
Those who have eyes, let them see.
Today is your day to receive wisdom.
What is wisdom?
The Holy Spirit leads us into all truth.
The teachings of men.
The origin of your theology.
The doctrine of demons.
You say you believe the Bible, why don't you believe it?
Apologetics? (Can you argue someone into Heaven?)
The Tree of Life.
The Tree of the Knowledge of Good & Evil.
The Two Trees & the Old and New Wine.
The Tree of the Knowledge of Good & Evil makes you like satan.
When we read the Bible, is there any priority to what we read? For instance, should we read more of what Paul wrote, or of what Jesus said?
Why does it seem like Paul wrote things that were contrary to each other in the Scriptures?

Besides what Paul wrote, there are other things written in Scripture that seem to oppose each other. Why?
What does 1 Corinthians 1:20 mean?
What does it mean to be "woke," and can a follower of Christ be "woke"?
Can a pastor really be woke?
What about ideologies? How do we know what's right to believe?
Can a good thing become a stronghold?
How do we decide if something like a "word" is from God or not?

Law of the Spirit
Do you believe that Jesus fulfilled the Law and the Prophets?
If the Law has been fulfilled, which part of the Law do you obey?
Do you get extra credit for obeying the law?
What is the law of the Spirit?
There is no condemnation for those in Christ Jesus.
The Holy Spirit invites you into a relationship.
Have you learned how to love?
Can you be patient today?
If you can see that I (the Lord) have been kind, could you also show kindness to those I love today?
Do you have jealousy in your heart?
Bragging doesn't come from Me.
Can you see that arrogance keeps your eyes on yourself?
The Old Testament explains the Old Covenant.
The New Testament explains the New Covenant.
Jesus is the Teacher of the New Covenant.
Why is it said that the New Covenant is a Covenant of Jesus' blood?
Explanation of the "Mercy Seat" and the blood.
Are there any of the Old Covenant Laws that must be followed by the New Covenant believer?
What does it mean to have the Law in our minds and in our hearts?
You only "win" by the Spirit, not by the intellect.

Prayer
How do you know what to pray?
What if you don't know what to pray?
Do not pray in agreement with your adversary.
The enemy disguises himself as an angel of light.
Anger, bitterness, and offense allows Satan to set the agenda.

What is God's agenda?
Is prayer asking for things or talking with God? (back and forth)
Ask Me how to pray.
Don't pray according to the wisdom of men.
Do pray according to His will and His agenda.
Is there another way to have peace?
What do you really expect from Me?
It's His desire to do what people are asking in prayer.
Does God inquire of men when He desires to do a thing?
What is there about prayer that brings joy?
Do you believe your prayer has power?

Love & Faith

My way is the way of love.
"The love of God compels me."
What is Love?
Well done good and faithful servant.
Pride: Have you reached your goal? Then help somebody else reach theirs.
Jesus: How did He help others reach their goal?
The Kingdom suffers violence.
Love does not act unbecomingly. Do you?
Love does not seek its own!
Are you easily provoked? Love isn't.
Love does not take into account a wrong suffered.
Love does not rejoice in unrighteousness.
Love rejoices in the truth!
Love bears all things.
Love believes all things.
Love hopes all things
Love endures all things.
*Love **never** fails.*
Love wins.
How should differences be settled between a husband and a wife?
How do believers settle disagreements, even when it involves Scripture?
Why do you want to keep going around that mountain?
Lift up your eyes.

Healing & Deliverance

Were there any demons who didn't bow to Jesus?
Where there any sicknesses that didn't leave when Jesus touched someone?
Can any Spirit-filled man, woman, or child cast out a spirit (demon)?
How do I know if a spirit needs to be cast out?
Do I have to know the name of the spirit in order to cast it out?
What if I think there's a spirit to cast out, but there really isn't?
What, exactly, do I say to cast out a demon?
How could the discerning of spirits gifting help in casting out a demon?
What was Paul's thorn in the flesh?

Discipleship

As He is, so are we in this world.
What does it look like to be as Jesus is in the world?
Did the devil ever win against Jesus?
All authority has been given to Me – so GO!
Freely you have received, freely give.
Don't throw your pearls to pigs.
Through trials and tribulations journey with Christ.
Suffering teaches obedience.
Suffer for doing good and not evil.
Suffering for Christ is NOT the fate of the unfortunate.
Look to the reward!
Count the Cost.
Life and death are in the tongue – Part 1.
Life and death are in the tongue – Part 2.
As a man thinks in his heart, so is he.
The only way you can bear fruit is to be connected to the vine.
Have you chosen the Good Vine?
You must choose.
The human will can be used to achieve greatness.
The human will can be lied to in such a way as to create doubt and unbelief.
The human will can be harnessed by hell to be extremely evil.
The human will can be lied to and frustrated to become addicted to virtually anything.
Anyone who wills to do My will becomes a new person.
If you will to do His will, you're set free to achieve your destiny.
I've given everyone a destiny, but they must will to follow it.
A person's destiny which I have given them is what they've always longed for or desired to do.

The longer a person is on a deviant path, the harder it is to come back to the correct course.
I give some over to their own desires.
Some are so deceived, that in their pride, they can't come back.
Come back to Me, and I'll come back to you.
Your desire is always for Me. (Some people just don't know it.)
True happiness cannot be found outside My will or desire for you.
Power forces a decision.
Spend time with Me. You'll never be disappointed that you did.
Stop, Look, Ask & Ask.
Boldness & Faith
A disciple evangelizes by default.
Being a true disciple flies in the face of religion.
Religion looks in. Disciples look out.
Power of self or power of God?
A disciple is comfortable with doing the impossible.
Disciples look at what God has to offer.
Looking at self is illegal for a disciple.
Disciples believe they can do what their Master does.
Disciples are not greater than their Master.
Why did the Lord choose the Apostle Paul to minister for Him? (Saul seems like he was really bad.)
Where did Paul learn to minister for the Lord?
What kind of resistance should we expect from our enemy?
Does resistance increase as we progress in our Christian walk?
How does religion play into the hands of our enemy against Spirit-filled believers?
Did Jesus have issues with the religious leaders of His time?
Why do the religious have issues with Spirit-filled believers?
How are we, as Spirit-filled believers, supposed to deal with this persecution?
Religion argues. Does the Spirit argue back?
Practice having faith that words will be put in your mouth.
The right answer is always Jesus.
As a follower of Jesus Christ, you will face perils. So, what does that mean?
What are vain imaginations?
Why would vain imaginations come into your mind?
Why are vain imaginations wrong for the Spirit-filled believer?
Should we ever argue or dispute?

Enter His gates with thanksgiving.
Enter His courts with praise!
Lift up holy hands.

The Church
Can the church be in truth without the Holy Spirit leading it?
The ecclesia is not housed in a building.
Without spot or wrinkle?
Apostolic Mandate
Prophetic Decree
Unity in the Spirit among the five-fold.
Agreement by the Holy Spirit in love.
Exclusivity of the Five-Fold.
Rejecting the gifts to the church?
The Five-Fold Ministers will be judged more harshly.
Those who come in His Name, whom He sends.
His Kingdom is a kingdom, not a republic or a democracy.
Father says, "Can you see that I put everything in My Son's hands?"
The church has to be according to the Son because of love.
If a church doesn't have life, it doesn't have Me. (Not The church, but a church.)
If a church has no life, then leave.
My Spirit is always moving.
My church is financed by Me, not by witchcraft.
Apostles and prophets lay the foundation.
Evangelists, pastors, and teachers do not have the privilege of generating theology.
Did Paul actually minister with Jesus? If not, that makes him a different kind of apostle, doesn't it?
The five-fold ministers lay down their lives to help the saints complete the vision God has for them.
The five-fold ministers are the Jesus way.
Jesus is the head of the church.
The church another way is not the church. He's the Way. It's His church.
How would someone with the Spirit of Christ settle differences with another follower of Jesus Christ?
Can unity be accomplished any other way than the Spirit of Christ?
There are so many ways that people have believed the Scriptures; is it possible for the Spirit of Christ to reconcile all of these?

How would your church accommodate a teen with the gift of prophecy?
What if a teen in your church is more anointed than the adults? What do you do?
Is there a spirit of pride in your church?
Does your church exist to make the congregants look good, or to lift Jesus ever higher?
If a teen was known to be a member of the five-fold, how would your church train him or her?
How does your church raise up teens in the gifts of the Spirit?
Teenagers separate from church because they're held separate from the church. "My Church is one."

Children
Should children be exposed to things like prophecy? Healing? Other power gifts of the Holy Spirit?
Is it a parent's decision when their child should experience baptism, gifts of the Spirit, etc.? Or is it God's decision?
Why would parents be upset if their child has an experience with the Lord (think baptism, born again, gifts of the Spirit, prophecy, etc.)?
How should we make decisions in parenting? By logic?
Could you take a word from the Lord if it came through a child?
Is it possible for parents to be in unity in raising children?
It's not about filtering out the bad; it's about freely releasing the good.
What does godly discipline look like?
Is it a benefit to know your child's destiny? Should you seek God on this? Perhaps ask a prophet?
Is there ever a time when a parent should stand in the way of something that the Holy Spirit wants to do for their child?
What should a parent expect or look for in a church for their children? Should the children participate in the same way as the adults?
Why is it common to teach children to be bystanders and not participants in church?
Do children's dreams, visions, and words have the same worth as adults?
Should parents pursue interpretation of their children's dreams, visions, words, etc.?
What do parents do if their child is having nightmares or seeing the demonic?
How do parents handle fear in a child?
How do parents decide what's appropriate for a teenager?

How should parents handle video games?
How should parents handle their teens' bad friends?
Should teens be separated from adults in church, teaching settings, other gatherings?
How do you raise your child to know good from evil and follow the good when they're teens?

www.ingramcontent.com/pod-product-compliance
Lightning Source LLC
Chambersburg PA
CBHW070832160426
43192CB00012B/2179